Music and Alzheimer's

Cognitive Behavior Modification Through Music

A Guide for Community Music Schools

Beverly Pickering

George Owens

Jason Trotta

Pamela Hamberg

MUSIC AND ALZHEIMER'S: Cognitive Behavior Modification Through Music

For further information, contact Northampton Community Music Center (www.ncmc.net) at (413) 585-0001.

Disclaimer:
The team who designed and implemented the Cognitive Behavior Modification Program through Music program in Northampton consulted medical professionals regularly about the residents involved. We recommend you do the same before implementing the program described in this manual or any variation of the approach we have offered. This manual is in no way intended to substitute for the advice and oversight of medical professionals.

We gratefully acknowledge **The F.A.O. Schwarz Family Foundation** for funding the Cognitive Behavior Modification Through Music Project and the publication of this guidebook.

Contents

Foreword

Dear Fellow Music School Directors:

I hope that the information contained in this manual will both help and inspire you to launch what could be one of the most memorable and rewarding projects of your career. I know that my own perception about the power of music has been forever changed by things I have witnessed during the past four years and I am excited by the prospect of seeing you, my colleagues and friends, continue to further this great work all across the country.

While most of the structures and procedures that we suggest in this book reflect exactly how we did things ourselves, some are the result of what we learned from our mistakes. We describe approaches that should yield the most success given the idiosyncrasies of typical community music school structures while also helping you minimize the sorts of challenges we faced in navigating this project for the first time.

The Northampton Community Music Center and I as its director were blessed to work directly in partnership with Beverly Pickering, whose cumulative knowledge, skills, and life experiences led to her conceiving of this project to begin with. She was never an employee of our school, but an equal partner who was engaged in all aspects of bringing this project to fruition, including finding and securing the required funding and running all of the music sessions.

Combinations of talents such as Beverly's are rare, however. In this book, we have defined a Music Program Coordinator position that would be filled by an employee of your school, whether this individual is a new-hire or an existing staff member. You as Executive Director will need to play a leading role in the program, which will mean you must become a quick study in the history and effects of Alzheimer's Disease, the phenomenon of "sundowning," and the research surrounding brain cell activity sparked by music. These areas of knowledge fall well outside the usual expertise of a music school director, but are essential in this case. Throughout the book we have identified specific resources that will help you learn more about these subjects and more.

If after reading this book, you feel you have the resources and desire to launch such a program at your school, I welcome and urge you to contact both Beverly and myself for advice and consultation. We would be thrilled to offer our combined insights and perspectives to help you create a program that hopefully surpasses even what we accomplished these past four years.

Sincerely,

Jason Trotta, Executive Director
Northampton Community Music Center

Chapter 1: Introduction

Chapter Goals

This chapter will provide you with an introduction to *Cognitive Behavior Modification Through Music*, including some references to the theoretical background for the program. We also explain this manual—what it is, how it was developed, and how you can use the process and tools we provide.

Objectives

The information and tools provided in this chapter will enable you to:
- Explain what a *Cognitive Behavior Modification Through Music* program is and how the approach was developed and tested
- Describe some of the basic theoretical foundation for the program
- Find additional resources to further educate yourself about music and brain function
- Begin to determine whether a *Cognitive Behavior Modification Through Music* program will be a good fit for your organization

The Foundation

According to the Alzheimer's Association (www.alz.org), an estimated 5.3 million Americans currently suffer from various stages of Alzheimer's Dementia. More and more of these individuals are living out their final years isolated in the residential units of underserved Medicare/ Medicaid nursing home facilities. Each of these individuals enters such a facility with significant cognitive impairment, only to face increasing mental and physical decline.

The round-the-clock demands of providing care to these residents leave no time for nursing staff to institute beneficial programs addressing cognition and behavior, especially at the "sundowning" time of day, when many residents experience heightened stress and anxiety. There is an urgent need for methods through which to transfer residents' negative energy and agitation into positive behavior and effective communication.

Recent research indicates previously unrecognized pathways in the brain that influence memory, behavior, and emotion. It is now possible to understand brain function as it relates to cognition, and to describe the network of neurological pathways receptive to creative stimulation. Music is widely acclaimed as one of the most powerful of all creative forces, with unlimited potential for clinical use.

Dr. Oliver Sacks, speaking of "those who are lost to dementia," says "music is no luxury to them but a necessity, and can have power beyond anything else to restore them to themselves, and to others, at least for a while."

Dr. Daniel Levitin states, "Music is clearly a means for improving people's moods. It also invokes some of the same neural regions that language does, but far more than language, music taps into primitive brain structures involved with motivation, reward, and emotion."

Dr. Gene Cohen notes, "The very act of engaging one's mind in creative ways affects health directly via the many mind/body connections. Our brains are deeply connected to our bodies via nerves, hormones, and the immune system. Anything that stimulates the brain, reduces stress, and promotes a more balanced emotional response will trigger positive changes in the body." Cohen also says that "the capacity to learn never dies…creativity is an emotional and intellectual process that can, moment by moment, displace negative feelings such as anxiety and hopelessness, with positive feelings of engagement and expectation."

The work of these three renowned researchers has provided the foundation for our efforts to convert scientific discoveries into vital clinical programs for everyday use. As you explore the idea of launching a Cognitive Music program, we strongly encourage you to read the works of all three and to investigate the other resources that we identify throughout this manual.

People Living with Alzheimer's

Throughout this manual, we refer to our audience as people living with Alzheimer's or as residents; we have intentionally avoided calling them patients whenever possible for several reasons. First, while they may have been patients of the nursing home, they were not **our** patients, nor should you as executive director of a community music school view participants in your own program as patients. The objectives of this program will be achievable only if the participants are viewed as an audience of experienced adults who must be related to seriously, with dignity, understanding, and trust in their capacity to receive the music and connect with others in return.

John Zeisel, author of *I'm Still Here* and president of Hearthstone Alzheimer Care, writes quite eloquently about ways of understanding and connecting with people living with Alzheimer's. We highly recommend his book as another important resource to help you consider and prepare for beginning the program we describe, and will quote him at length here.

Zeisel writes, "A person living with Alzheimer's is first "a person" and only then someone with a disease. The way the world sees Alzheimer's today is that a person is almost totally lost once he or she receives an Alzheimer's diagnosis—lost both to themselves and to those who love them. An Alzheimer's diagnosis is seen as an Alzheimer's "sentence." But this just isn't so."

Later he says, "Another inaccurate perception is that when people are diagnosed with Alzheimer's they have no future—that an Alzheimer's diagnosis is an Alzheimer's sentence. The condition lasts ten to fifteen years, a time span that definitely constitutes a future. "What kind of future is it if people can't remember their children and where they are?" those who don't understand the disease ask. That question assumes that memories are gone, which they are not, they are just increasingly inaccessible without some help. It also assumes that the future is based in the past and in past memories. It is not. The future is based on many present moments—moments the person experiences fully every day and every minute.

"If we rely primarily on drugs to alleviate the symptoms of Alzheimer's—or what most people assume to be those symptoms—there is little available treatment at present. Some cognitive enhancement drugs have some effects; many have side effects. Some mood drugs can reduce disturbing behaviors, often at the price of reduced quality of life...*Nonpharmacological* environmental and behavioral treatments can have dramatic results with few side effects. Symptoms that everyone thought were integral to the disease can be reduced...What many people assume are symptoms of the disease are not actually symptoms—they're often reactions to caregiving, social environment, medical treatment, and physical environment."

Our observations clearly demonstrate that music, especially when provided for residents during "sundowning" time, can help counteract many of the negative effects of Alzheimer's disease, especially those stemming from the reactions to external conditions that Zeisel describes.

The Role of Community Music Schools

Over the past several decades, community music schools have proliferated throughout the country. As their name implies, many of these organizations include connections within the community as an important part of their core mission. Many actively seek opportunities for their students to perform in public, especially in venues outside the school itself, both to build student skills and confidence and to bolster the school's visibility and ties to the community.

Similarly, many Alzheimer's facilities have either a regulatory requirement or a mission obligation to make sure their residents maintain some ties with the community outside the facility. This is often difficult, because of the combination of limited resources and the potentially counter-productive and destabilizing effect of removing people living with Alzheimer's from familiar surroundings without adequate support.

A community-based partnership between music centers and Alzheimer's facilities is a natural and obvious fit, with clear benefits for both. Before we began our project, however, we were unable to find any existing examples of similar collaborations that we could use as models for our own program. That led us to explore how we could build our own.

A Brief History of Our Program

In the fall of 2006, Beverly Pickering combined her interests as a professional pianist with an RN degree, and approached Jason Trotta, Executive Director of the Northampton Community Music Center (NCMC), and Pamela Hamberg, Geriatric Program Director of the 41 person Rockwell Alzheimer's Dementia residential unit at Northampton Rehabilitation & Nursing Center, with an idea to partner the two agencies in creating a multi-generational Cognitive Behavior Modification Through Music pilot study project. The group sought funding and was awarded a grant by the F.A.O. Schwarz Family Foundation. In January, 2008, NCMC initiated a 20-week project, "Cognitive Behavior Modification Through Music," in partnership with the Northampton Rehabilitation and Nursing Center. This unique study sought to study the possible effect of live music performances on problems of memory retrieval, recollection, thought, behavior, and quality of life during the "sundowning" time of day in middle to late-stage Alzheimer's residents.

Faculty and students of the Northampton Community Music Center presented forty-two performance sessions during the five month period of the study (January to May, 2008). A second grant from F.A.O. Schwarz Family Foundation, enabled us to conduct eighty-five more music sessions between November, 2008 and July, 2009. The more than three hundred visiting musicians varied in age and experience from 4 to 94 years, and the genres of music and instrumentation covered during the nine month period were extremely diverse.

**A Brief
History of
Our
Program,
cont'd.**

We developed tools for observational and medical documentation and used them during and after each session. Observation by those responsible for the residents' daily care and by those involved in running the program or performing revealed the extent to which music inspired positive thinking and behavior in the residents. For all of those involved, the results demonstrated the value of music as a tool for cognitive treatment and improving the quality of life of the residents.

One of the most obvious differences, readily observed by staff and musicians alike, was the audience's change in attention span from ten to fifteen minutes at the beginning of the program to fully forty-five minutes by the conclusion of the second year.

Beverly noted a memorable day when she walked through the front doors of the nursing center and she heard a voice call to her, "Missy! Missy! Are we going to have music at 3:30 this afternoon?" It was one of the residents of the Alzheimer's Dementia unit.

**Some
Results
Observed
from Our
Project**

Some of the most revealing observations about the effects of music on our participants come from the staff of the Alzheimer's facility where we developed and ran our program. These are the people who interacted daily with all of the residents and were best able to detect changes in cognition, mood, and behavior.

Brenda Colon, an Activities Assistant, wrote "In my opinion the music grant program is like a miracle for all our residents…There are many times after the music is over and they are back in the unit, that I hear some of them singing or humming the songs from the concert. They also tell me that they really enjoyed it and even mention how they used to dance to such and such a song, and how it brings back memories (even for a short time) of times past when they were young and carefree."

The Alzheimer's Resident Unit Manager, Jennifer Wade, L.P.N., said, "I have noted some positive results with some residents regarding usage of psychotic medications. Some residents have tolerated a medication reduction or even been completely taken off their anti-psychotic medication." She also noted, "There has been an increase in appetite after performances with no unplanned weight loss since the grant (*our project*) started." And she summarized by saying, "I see a positive outcome with music in the Alzheimer's Dementia residents, especially with sundowning." (*Ms. Wade is referring to the cognitive and behavioral challenges people living with Alzheimer's often face at sundowning time, which we will discuss later in this manual.*)

Some Results Observed from Our Project, cont'd.

Josie Zawada, the Assistant Activities Coordinator and a Certified Nursing Assistant (C.N.A.) at the facility, attended all of the sessions and closely observed the responses of the residents. She said that, "Music brings them into their own world with better mood and longer conversations with peers. Some became more alert and polite. The music decreased their anxiety and helped them feel part of a group. I hear more comments from them like "I love you" and "Thank you." This is all new for these residents."

Jessica Arsenault, and Activities Assistant and C.N.A., wrote "I see a big difference compared to before the music grant came. Sociability and warmth has increased. The variety of music reaches everybody. There is a change in ambience and residents show more awareness. They have more creativity and are able to connect better. Human contact and familiarity with one another has grown. It shows a lot."

The visiting musicians unanimously came away from this project with a sense of enlightenment and a strong desire to return. Putting the power of music to clinical use in our community is fast becoming part of the culture of NCMC, and we are all grateful to the F.A.O. Schwarz Family Foundation for the opportunity to launch such a worthwhile endeavor.

Much more detail on the methods and findings of our project is available in the final reports for each grant, which are available on the Northampton Community Music Center website: www.ncmc.net/specialproject.html

Introduction to the Program

Now let's consider some basic information and definitions. Then we'll discuss the purpose and use of this manual.

<u>What is a *Cognitive Behavior Modification through Music* program?</u>

The program is a music/medical partnership designed to enhance cognitive abilities and improve behavior of patients with middle to late stage Alzheimer's dementia. It works by providing diverse but consistent stimulation through frequent live musical performances at a time of day when many patients are typically experiencing the most negative aspects of their ailment, i.e., "sundowning time," the late afternoon hours. At many facilities, this is a time of day when patients don't get much attention, although they may well need it most during these hours. The relative lack of attention is usually due to logistics—staff shifts normally change during these hours, and patients are left to rest while outgoing staff completes paperwork and the incoming shift comes up to speed on patient status. Music reaches deeply into the minds of these patients, especially during these vulnerable hours, and a *Cognitive Behavior Modification through Music* program can become a significant component of medical treatment, providing an upgrade in treatment and care that results in observable improvements in patients' quality of life.

<u>Why should your Music Center consider a *Cognitive Behavior Modification through Music* program? What will be the benefits?</u>

This is the type of program that is central to the core mission of many Community Music Schools because it so clearly uses music to promote connection and healing in a broader social setting for an underserved audience, while also fostering the overall education of students. Not only do the performances build student skills and confidence—the sessions also create a very real and quite instantly enlightening understanding of the broader importance and impact of music. Students see first-hand that music is not only something done at home or school for one's own enjoyment, or in performance merely as a personal accomplishment, but that it's an activity that when shared can do some very real good for others.

Also, we have found that these performances build relationships between musicians that are very different from other types of rehearsals and performances—students see the immediate connection and impact of the music they're creating together, and they talk about it amongst themselves afterwards, and we've seen how motivating this can be.

And finally, in an even larger sense, programs such as this help to bridge generations in the community, not an insignificant accomplishment in a time when families can be more geographically dispersed and when the young and the elderly may have little daily contact with each other.

Introduction to the Program, cont'd.

How is *Cognitive Behavior Modification through Music* different from an entertainment program?

This program differs from normal entertainment programs or activities in both its scope and its intent. In terms of scope, the program involves frequent performances (a minimum of two per week, three recommended) by a large and diverse group of musicians, with a predictable structure (beginning and ending songs) and varied content in between. And the intent is quite purposeful, because this program is specifically designed to stimulate patients' mental activities in such a way as to build new connections and behaviors. When implemented as we have designed it, the program becomes a recurring, planned, managed part of patient care.

How is *Cognitive Behavior Modification through Music* different from music therapy?

Wherever music therapy is available at Alzheimer's facilities (it's a limited resource for many), it is of course a valuable and useful component of patient care. The music therapist is only one person, though, and may be called upon to work one-on-one with many patients or with very small groups. Community Music Schools can offer a very diverse range of peformers, representing all ages (we have had performers ranging in age from 4 to 94), many different instruments, and a very wide range of music. By using this program structure, we can provide patients with a much broader variety of mental stimulation much more frequently, with potentially much more impact. And doing so won't require special training on the part of the performers.

What resources and commitments will be required from the Community Music School?

The most important commitment required from you will be a dedicated person who can coordinate the program, including recruiting teachers and their students and musicians from outside the music school, scheduling performances, taking care of any logistics involved in transporting students, instruments, and equipment to and from the Alzheimer's facility, etc. If your Community Music School has an Outreach Coordinator, this work will be a natural extension of that person's role. Or you may have another staff member who could fulfill this function. Other possibilities that we have seen work include an intern from a local college, who works either for credit or pay through work-study, a musican connected to the school who has a relative in the facility, or a high-functioning resident at the same facility. The latter may be someone who resides in an assisted living area of the facility, and may be a musician herself, or someone with a long-standing interest in coordinating volunteer activities, or even a business or nursing background. Be creative in your thinking here, because many people will find the program very engaging and worthwhile and will be willing to step up and play an important role.

Introduction to the Program, cont'd.

<u>What should be the role of the Community Music School's Executive Director?</u>
Beyond completing the initial research and verifying the school's interest, identifying a partnering facility, and identifying and committing the time of a program coordinator, the Community Music School's Executive Director must be willing to assume an ongoing responsibility for promoting the program both internally and externally. Daily coordination of the program would usually require too much time given the Executive Director's many other responsibilities. A regular time commitment is essential, though, to keep selling the value of the program to teachers and students, whether in faculty meetings or individual interactions, until the program becomes a regular and naturally assumed part of the school's language, culture, and expectations. The Executive Director should also play a leading role in reaching out to the community for additional resources to support the program, including funding and musicians. The program should be promoted throughout the director's network and in local schools and colleges. We can't emphasize the importance of these activities enough: without the Executive Director's continuing, enthusiastic support and promotion, the program probably won't succeed.

<u>What will be the challenges for your Community Music School when implementing a *Cognitive Behavior Modification through Music* program?</u>
One of the most important challenges that we have identified will be how you engage your teachers in this program when, to put it bluntly, it will come at least partly out of their own pockets. In order to be effective, the performances need to take place at "sundowning" time. These late afternoon hours are normally prime hours for music lessons, and if the teachers are performing rather than teaching, they're giving up income. We have found several ways to deal with this issue. First, and most obvious, you can seek funding to provide a stipend for the teachers that will at least partially offset any income loss. Sources for this could include foundation funding, local businesses, or even the Alzheimer's facility itself. Second, some teachers already work with small groups of students, such as Suzuki classes, vocal groups, chamber music ensembles, and so on, and those teachers may be able to have their students perform during the normal class hour occasionally. And third, try to get as many different teachers as you can to perform at least once, so they can experience the impact of the program directly. Some will be so moved by and so appreciative of the response to their music that they will volunteer as often as they can. We have seen this happen, and these musicians have been among the finest and staunchest contributors to the program.

Introduction to the Program, cont'd.

<u>What resources and commitments will be required from the Alzheimer's facility?</u>

Our expectations of the Alzheimer's facility are covered in detail in Chapter 3 of this manual. Briefly, the main requirements will be these:

- A commitment to host 2-3 performances per week at sundowning time
- A consistent, appropriate space for the performances
- Ability to have residents prepared and accompanied by aides as needed for every performance
- Enthusiasm and support from all key personnel

<u>When should you NOT consider implementing a program?</u>

It may be readily apparent when you should not attempt to implement one of these programs. We have identified a number of factors that should warn you to consider the decision very carefully:

- When there is not broad support within your school, from faculty and the Board
- When you are unable to find a facility within reasonable travel distance that is willing to partner with you, or the facility cannot commit to at least 2-3 performances per week during sundowning time
- When the program does not fit into your school's mission or strategic plan
- When the school's faculty is not generally supportive or cooperative with outreach programs (sadly, this is true at some schools)
- When you are unable to identify a person who can commit the time required to coordinate the program
- When you don't have a strong network of musicians from the community outside the school who are willing to volunteer for performances

<u>What external resources might be available to help support the program?</u>

We believe that three main categories of outside resources will help you succeed: money (though not a great deal may be required), musicians, and publicity.

First the money. You may want to seek outside funding in order to support a program coordinator, to provide stipends to teachers, or to offset transportation or other logistical costs. We strongly suggest that you consider not only foundation grants, but also local businesses who may be interested in attaching their name to such a very specific, visible, and praiseworthy program.

Now the musicians. Two or three performances every week for months will require quite a few musicians. And the more diverse the music, the more beneficial the program can be. You'll have regulars, of course, who engage with the program and want to play a continuing role. But you'll need a wide pool of talent to draw from. We have found many local musicians who have

Introduction to the Program, cont'd.

been very interested in volunteering, especially when we have created an existing structure and venue and all they need to do is show up and play. In many cases, these musicians have been friends of teachers, parents of students, or simply other musicians in the community who heard about the program and wanted to participate. Cast a wide net, spread the word, contact local schools and colleges. Beyond recruiting musicians for this program, you will expand your Community Music School's network and pool of contacts, and possibly even identify some new teachers and bring in some new students!

Once the program is under way, local publicity will be very important for helping you build participation of musicians and sponsors alike. You're probably quite familiar with the normal channels for publicity in your community through your every day responsibilities as Executive Director. Think beyond the local newspaper, radio, TV, and arts magazines, though, and involve your local chapter of the Alzheimer's Association. (You can identify them through www.alz.org) They may be able to help you channel your publicity in new directions.

What is the purpose of this manual?

This manual is intended to help Community Music Schools and Alzheimer's facilities throughout the U.S. plan and implement *Cognitive Behavior Modification through Music* programs. We provide a great deal of very practical "how-to" information that is based on our experience designing, running, and evaluating a pilot program in Northampton, Massachusetts over a two-year period.

Along the way, we include some relevant theory and background information from some of the major researchers in the field, but this manual is not a textbook. Wherever we can, we point you to more in-depth background information, such as books, articles, and websites.

Our overall purpose is to help spread the very real and exciting benefits of what we've learned while conducting frequent live music performances at sundowning time for people living with Alzheimer's.

Who is the audience?

The primary audience for this manual is anyone who will be responsible for decision-making, planning, and implementation of a *Cognitive Behavior Modification through Music* program. At minimum this means Executive Directors (or equivalent senior administrative titles) at Community Music Schools. Others who may find the information quite useful will be members of the Board of Directors, other Community Music School administrators and faculty, and Alzheimer's facility administrators, especially Geriatric Program Directors and Activities Directors.

How was this manual developed?

This manual was developed by the team that designed and implemented the pilot *Cognitive Behavior Modification through Music* program in Northampton, Massachusetts, between 2006 and 2009, including
- Pamela Hamberg, Geriatric Program Director, Northampton Rehabilitation & Nursing Center
- Beverly Pickering, Music Specialist/RN, Northampton Community Music Center
- Jason Trotta, Executive Director, Northampton Community Music Center

Design and writing of the manual was provided by
- George Owens, Writer/Training Consultant (and one of the many musicians who participated in the program)

Funding for both the program and for development and printing of this manual was provided through the generous support of the F.A.O. Schwarz Family Foundation, to whom we extend our most profound thanks and gratitude.

How can this manual be used?

This manual is intended to support practical, hands-on application. Each chapter covers a major stage or component of the program. For each stage, we provide an overview, information about the key people who need to be involved and the support that will be required from them, and the major steps involved. We give you some tips and cautions, based on our own experience. And, we include sample tools, such as checklists, letters, orientation materials, etc., that you can use as-is or tailor to your own needs. Finally, each chapter provides references for additional information.

We strongly recommend that you read this entire manual before actually beginning to initiate any planning or work on a program. That will give you a realistic idea of the tasks and people that should be involved, and you'll have a much better sense of whether the program will be feasible for your Community Music School.

Next Steps

1. Educate yourself! The most valuable and germane resources that we have found are listed below. Read these books!

2. Read the next chapter of this manual, Planning, to learn how to assess whether a *Cognitive Behavior Modification through Music* program will be appropriate and feasible for your Community Music Center and, if it appears to be, to help you begin planning for implementation of a successful program.

References

Books

Cohen, Gene D., *The Mature Mind, The Positive Power Of The Aging Brain*, Basic Books, 2005. www.creativeaging.org

Cohen, Gene D., *The Creative Age, Awakening Human Potential In The Second Half Of Life*, Harper Collins Publishers, 2000. www.creativeaging.org

Levitin, Daniel J., *This Is Your Brain On Music*, Plume Books, 2007. www.yourbrainonmusic.com

Sacks, Oliver, *Musicophilia*, Vintage Books, 2008. http://musicophilia.com

Zeisel, John, *I'm Still Here*, Avery, 2009. http://ImStillHere.org

Websites

McGovern Institute for Brain Research at MIT
http://web.mit.edu/mcgovern

Society for the Arts in Health Care
http://www.thesah.org

Chapter 2: Planning

Chapter Goals

Our goals in this chapter are to enable you to determine whether a *Cognitive Behavior Modification through Music* program will be appropriate and feasible for your Community Music School and to help you begin planning for implementation of a successful program.

Objectives

The information and tools provided in this chapter will help you:
- Explain the major steps involved in planning and implementing a *Cognitive Behavior Modification through Music* program
- Anticipate program costs
- Assess the level of interest and support within your organization
- Decide whether to move forward with identifying a potential partner Alzheimer's facility
- Identify a Music Program Coordinator

Overview

By choosing to implement a *Cognitive Behavior Modification through Music* program, you will be providing an enormously valuable resource for your community and an enriching, potentially life-changing, experience for the teachers and students associated with your school. A successful program will demand a major commitment of time and energy; this chapter provides some steps and tools you can use to help determine whether this program will be a good fit for your school.

Overview, cont'd.	Use this chapter to learn about the preliminary concerns and the overall steps related to building a program. Subsequent chapters provide more detail in specific areas, such as identifying a partnering facility, recruiting and training musicians, selecting music, running the actual performance sessions, and so on. Before you immerse yourself in those particulars, though, it will be helpful to understand the overall requirements.

The most significant precondition that must be in place before you find an Alzheimer's facility with which to work is an <u>enthusiastic</u> level of support within your school. Passion about music and community service is crucial! Mild interest on the part of the board of directors, staff, or teachers won't be enough to sustain the program, even if you're able to get it up and running.

The Community Music School's Executive Director may need to stoke the enthusiasm by educating everyone about the program: what it is, how it will benefit people with Alzheimer's and musicians and the school, and what it will require. |
| **Criteria for deciding to proceed with finding a partner** | Before you expend the time and effort necessary to identify and screen local Alzheimer's facilities as potential partners, make very sure that you

- Have enthusiastic support from your school's Board of Directors
- Have or can acquire the financial resources necessary to support a person dedicated at least half-time to running the program for at least the first six months
- Can identify the <u>right</u> person to run the program; this individual must have a very special set of skills
- Have teachers who are willing to perform (on their own and/or with their students) during hours when they might otherwise be teaching

If you can't meet **all four** of those basic requirements, you should invest more time in building support, gaining funding, and identifying a program administrator before you begin to seek out an Alzheimer's facility. |

Pros & Cons of Working with Current Facilities

Your school may already have a musical relationship with one or more local nursing homes through existing outreach efforts, perhaps at facilities where your students perform at holidays or other special occasions. If one of these relationships is a particularly good one, and you have a close contact at the facility who would be supportive of a more formal and intensive program for its residents living with Alzheimer's, this might be a selling point for you internally. Rather than being an abstract and perhaps complicated concept, this program may seem to be a more natural and easily accomplished objective because it could be a more structured expansion of an existing and ongoing effort.

Remember, though, that the goals of a *Cognitive Behavior Modification through Music* program go far beyond entertainment. You will be working intensively with a group of people living with Alzheimer's dementia to improve their cognitive abilities and behavior. Occasional performances at nursing homes for a large audience serve a very different (and worthwhile!) purpose, but this program will be quite different in its aims and the level of commitment.

When you are implementing a new program such as this, making the very clear distinction may be difficult, both internally at your music school and at the facility. You will need to push hard to make sure that this program is conceptualized accurately. You must communicate clearly about the goals and structure of the program in order to get past the preconceived notions that many people may have about music providing only entertainment.

Key People & Required Support

During the planning phase, you will need to seek support from throughout your Community Music School.

- The Executive Director will normally be responsible for initiating consideration of the program and investigating feasibility and researching potential funding, then presenting the concept to the Board and Faculty, answering their questions, and ascertaining their level of support.

- The Board of Directors will usually be involved in helping the Executive Director make the decision on whether or not to proceed with a *Cognitive Behavior Modification through Music* program. Their considerations will most likely include factors such as the Community Music School's:
  - overall mission and strategy
  - financial condition
  - size (i.e., does the school have large enough faculty and student population to be able to launch and sustain a program such as this)
  - other (existing or planned) commitments for community outreach (Board members may have strong preferences)
  - staff capabilities

Key People & Required Support, cont'd.

- <u>Administrative Staff</u> may play a variety of roles, depending on the Community Music School. Some larger schools already have an Outreach Coordinator (or similar position) who is responsible for providing musical services to the larger community. A *Cognitive Behavior Modification through Music* program will be a natural extension of this person's job, and she or he might take a leading role in advocating for the program and developing the relationship. Other schools have smaller staffs, sometimes overworked, who may initially see this program as an additional project involving a great deal of work. In these situations, it will be very important to sell the benefits of the program to the school (as described in Chapter 1) and to make sure that you will be able to fund and identify an additional person who will run the program. Adding administration of this intensive program to a staff already stretched thin will be a sure path to failure.

- <u>Faculty</u> should be enlisted early in your planning process. You are probably already aware of at least a few who will be strong supporters. We have already discussed in Chapter 1 how dependent your success will be on the enthusiastic cooperation of your school's teachers. A few enthusiastic faculty members can help spread the message and bring others on board.

  You can educate your faculty about this program by providing them with copies of this manual. You may also want to buy copies of the books by Gene Cohen, Daniel Levitin, Oliver Sacks, David Shenk, and John Zeisel that are listed as references at the end of Chapter 1 and circulate these among your staff. Or you may identify other relevant articles, either through this manual or your own research. The most important point is to share information as you consider the project and build support as you go.

**Key People
& Required
Support,
cont'd.**

- <u>Music Therapist</u>—Many Community Music Schools have a trained music therapist on the faculty or staff, and questions may arise about why this program does not need to be run by a music therapist when the program clearly uses music for therapeutic purposes. Several major characteristics distinguish this program from most musical therapy.

  - First, this program has a *broader aim*, in that it works not exclusively as therapy for the audience, but also as a very important educational and community-building tool for teachers, students, parents, additional performers, and facility staff. The resources that support this program are the collective community, rather than a single trained individual. Many different parts of the community are able to contribute within the program's framework without a requirement of special individual training. The program also educates students about the power of music beyond what they probably think about while practicing and taking lessons. These performances go far beyond entertainment alone, and will encourage students, their parents, and probably their teachers to think about music in a new way.

  - Second, this program provides the listeners with a much *wider variety and greater frequency of musical stimulation* than an individual music therapist could provide. By bringing in so many different performers, instruments, and songs, you will be providing the residents with an extraordinarily enriching experience.

  - Third, this program certainly *does not exclude the music therapist*, nor is it intended to replace the work (or displace the job) of a music therapist. Instead, this program will enable the music therapist to focus much more on individual cases and residents throughout the facility. Many nursing and rehab centers include residents with a very wide range of conditions and needs, sometimes even including pediatric units, and the services of a music therapist are needed by more people. Given the tight budgets at most facilities, the music therapist gains more freedom to target her or his limited time to those with the greatest individual needs.

  In our program in Northampton, the music therapist who teaches at the Community Music School was involved in the program as one of the regular performers.

Overview of Steps

For planning purposes, here is an overview of the major steps you should take from the time you begin considering a *Cognitive Behavior Modification through Music* program up through the time the program is under way. All of these steps are covered in more detail elsewhere in this manual.

1. Educate yourself by reading this manual and the background materials recommended in Chapter 1
2. Assess Music School interest and support from staff, board, teachers, and students by presenting and explaining the benefits and structure
3. Determine budget required, seek external funding sources if necessary (a basic Budget Planning Worksheet is provided at the end of this chapter)
4. Select Music Program Coordinator (will require a very special person-- see Position Description at the end of this chapter)
5. Identify Alzheimer's facility for partnership and reach agreement (see Chapter 3)
6. Work with facility staff to identify small group of residents for pilot project (see Chapter 4)
7. Provide orientation to Music School teachers & identify who will participate (see Chapter 5)
8. Communicate with parents of students to educate them about the program (see Chapter 5)
9. Provide orientation to Alzheimer's facility staff (see Chapter 3)
10. Schedule initial performances (Should be a pilot period or "shakedown cruise" that uses experienced performers to smaller audience for limited number of performances (we suggest at least the first 4 weeks) in order to work out all the logistics and make sure everyone understands their responsibilities—see Chapter 7)
11. Meet regularly with Geriatric Program Director & facility staff to discuss and resolve any issues (see Chapter 7)
12. Expand audience and roster of performers (see Chapters 7 & 8)
13. Monitor and record behavior of audience members (see Chapter 9)
14. Hold monthly group meetings with teachers and other interested performers to share experiences and ideas and help grow and sustain the program (see Chapter 10). These meetings could be part of regular faculty meetings or separate meetings entirely.
15. Compile and report your results at regular, pre-determined intervals to the school's Board of Directors and any funding sources (see Chapter 9)
16. Develop a plan for sustaining the program long-term (see Chapter 10)

Cautions
- Make sure that you have established strong and enthusiastic support within your Community Music School before approaching facilities. As you present the program, you should assess constantly how people are responding to make sure you're getting lots of positive energy back. If you're feeling negativity within the school before you even begin setting up the program, this should be a major red flag and you should either adjust how you're communicating or rethink your plans to proceed.
- Make sure you understand and communicate the difference between this program and existing outreach and music therapy programs.

Tips
- Finding the right person to fill the role of Music Program Coordinator will be one of your most critical tasks. The position requires strong musical abilities (piano and voice), excellent administrative skills, and a talent for warm and supportive communication.

- Make sure that your message about the program is consistent, communicated widely and frequently within the school.

- Your enthusiasm is essential, but also make sure you balance it with reasonable expectations for the program.

Tools & Forms
- Music Program Coordinator Position Description
- Budget planning worksheet

References   One good source for researching possible funding sources is the Society for Arts in Health Care (www.thesah.org)

POSITION DESCRIPTION

JOB TITLE: Music Program Coordinator for *Cognitive Behavior Modification through Music* program

BASIC JOB DESCRIPTION:
Serve as principal liaison between the Community Music School and the Alzheimer's facility. Coordinate the planning, scheduling, and logistics for all live music performances presented at the selected partnering Alzheimer's facility. Attend and facilitate all performances, including assisting with setup and cleanup and performing opening and closing numbers. Monitor and report on overall program status. Reports to Community Music School Executive Director.

Typical duties/responsibilities may include, but are not limited to, the following:

- Participate in identification and selection of the Alzheimer's facility.
- Work closely with Music School Executive Director to identify and recruit teachers and musicians from the community.
- Schedule and conduct orientation sessions for musicians and facility staff.
- Work closely with Geriatric Program Director and Activities Director to identify residents for participation.
- Schedule all performances and communicate schedules to musicians and facility.
- Open and close every performance with standard songs. (Requires strong piano and voice performance ability.)
- Introduce musicians at the beginning of each performance.
- Intervene if performances aren't going well.
- Secure feedback from musicians after every performance.
- Provide feedback to musicians after every performance. Identify musicians who are most well-received and cultivate for repeat performances.
- Communicate regularly with Community Music School Executive Director about program status.

COMPLEXITY OF TASKS:
Requires the ability to manage multiple tasks, often under deadline. Requires strong organizational, time management, communication, and negotiating skills. Requires musical ability and great comfort in performing standard repertoire.

TYPICAL QUALIFICATIONS:
Bachelors Degree (in Music, Music Education, or Neuroscience, Biology, Psychology, etc., PLUS a strong background in music) and 3 to 5 years experience in a demanding, fast-paced administrative position.

HOURS:
Minimum of 20 hours per week, including performance times plus an hour before and after each; additional administrative hours will be flexible.

Budget Planning Worksheet

Anticipated costs to Community Music School for *Cognitive Behavior Modification through Music* program

Item	Description	Annual cost
Music Program Coordinator	Salary & benefits for half-time position	
Teacher stipends	Amount per performance x estimated number of performances	
Music	Sheet music, books, etc.	
Transportation	Costs for transporting students to and from the facility	
Equipment	Music stands; microphone & speaker if facility can't provide; etc. May also include rhythm instruments, shakers, etc., for use by residents	
Overhead (Portion of general administrative costs)		
TOTAL Estimated Cost		

Chapter 3: The Alzheimer's Facility

Chapter Goals

Our goals in this chapter are to enable you to select the Alzheimer's unit in your area that will be the best match for your Cognitive Behavior Modification through Music program and to help you prepare the facility's personnel for a successful launch of the program.

Objectives

The information and tools provided in this chapter will help you:
- identify potential partnering facilities for a cognitive music program
- gauge a facility's general level of need for a cognitive music program
- identify key personnel at the facility whose involvement will be necessary for success
- determine the potential level of support for a cognitive music program
- select the best candidate Alzheimer's unit
- provide an orientation for facility staff who will be affected by the program

Overview

The single most important element affecting successful implementation of a Cognitive Behavior Modification through Music program will be the facility that you select as your partner in the program. You should consider two critical factors: the level of need and the potential level of support from management.

Overview, cont'd.

Rather than finding the easiest facility for implementing the program, we suggest you seek out the facility where you can have the greatest impact. This usually means the facility with the greatest need, which will often be a facility that is struggling financially and unable to provide many offerings to residents beyond the most basic care. Signs of need can include a low or non-existent activities budget, little or no organized volunteer activities, low staffing/high turnover, and a neglected or poorly maintained physical setting.

Of course the level of need is only one factor. Beyond that, you must have a high level of interest, enthusiasm, and support for your program from all levels of management. You will need to assess this support before committing to implementing the program.

After you have identified the best facility and reached an agreement with them, you will need to provide some orientation for the facility's staff so that they can understand the very real benefits of the program. Staff who are responsible for the day to day care of residents may resist or resent the program because they initially view it as creating more work for them. Even staff who are not directly involved may have a negative reaction that gets communicated to others. You can greatly reduce this initial resistance and its possible impact on your success by providing an orientation before the program launches. Additional training will also be necessary for staff who work directly with the people living with Alzheimer's. We discuss that more in a later chapter.

Criteria for Selecting a Facility

Here are the most important criteria we have identified for selecting an appropriate Alzheimer's unit for a Cognitive Behavior Modification through Music program.

- Facility has a secluded/locked unit with residents in middle to late stages of Alzheimer's (Individuals scored at 4-6 on GDS scale, re-evaluted quarterly For more information, see Chapter 4: Your Audience).
- Low level of existing programs for Alzheimer's residents.
- Enthusiasm and support from key personnel.
- Availability of consistent appropriate space for performances.
- Willingness to make basic financial commitment (or seek donation) for acquisition and maintenance of piano, mic & speaker, music stands.
- Ability to commit to a minimum of 2 performances per week at sundowning time (Three is ideal.) NOTE: If the facility is unable to manage three weekly performances at sundowning time, scheduling one performance per week in the morning will also work acceptably. A minimum of two per week must be scheduled during sundowning for the program to have an impact on behavior and cognition, however.
- Facility within reasonable travel time for performers.
- Non-profit facilities may offer some advantages in terms of availability of external funding to support the program.

**Key People
& Required
Support**

In order to identify an appropriate Alzheimer's unit, you will need to meet with people who occupy these positions (or their functional equivalents) and determine how supportive each will be in their particular area.

Geriatric Program Director: This individual will most often be your first point of contact to assess interest and support for the program at a particular facility. The Geriatric Program Director has overall responsibility for the care and well-being of residents in the Alzheimer's unit. Without the support of this individual, there is little chance of your program succeeding. Beyond providing initial support and approval, the Geriatric Program Director will also be instrumental in selecting residents to participate in the program, training staff, and assuring overall staff support of the program. If the center is interested in tracking and documenting the results of the program, the Geriatric Program Director may also need to secure family permission for resident participation.

Activities Director: The Activities Director should also be an early contact when you are trying to identify a participating facility. This individual has overall responsibility for identifying, scheduling, and managing all activities offered to residents. The support and active participation of the Activities Director will be critical to your success. The Activities Director will most likely be the person involved in all of the day to day details of running the performances, including setting up and cleaning up the performance space, helping to greet and prepare performers, making sure residents have been prepared correctly ahead of time (medications, toileting, dress, etc. See Chapter 4: Your Audience, and Chapter 7: Running the Sessions, for more information about this aspect.)

Director of Nursing: Once you have the support and approval of the Geriatric Program Director and the Activities Director, they should help you in securing approval for the program from the Director of Nursing, who has overall responsibility for all day-to-day care. The Director of Nursing manages all health care aides, such as CNAs, and will be instrumental in making sure that normal Activities of Daily Living (ADLs) will not conflict with performances. The Director of Nursing may also be called upon to participate in participant selection and interface with families and care providers and to communicate to all staff the importance of the program to the Center's mission.

Facility Administrator: This individual has overall responsibility for running the facility, and must be willing to commit the necessary staff time and the space, and to meet any financial commitments that may be required. The Administrator handles employee conflicts, hiring and firing, budgets, and deals with overseeing authorities, regulations, etc.

Key People & Required Support, cont'd.

Other contacts at specific facilities may include the **Medical Director**, who may wish to be kept informed about individual participation and who may need to be consulted about medication or ongoing behavior issues, etc. You may also need to interact with the **Food Service Manager** for two main reasons: first, scheduling performance at sundowning time may have an impact on dining schedules for some residents; and second, at many facilities, the dining area may be a multiple use room that will also double as your performance space. In this case, the room will need to be rearranged before and after each performance, and this will also affect dining schedules.

Major Steps

1. First, EDUCATE yourself about the potential benefits of music for people living with Alzheimer's Dementia before you begin to contact facilities. One important step is to make sure that you have read and understood this entire manual before initiating contacts with nursing homes. You should also read as many related articles and books as possible; we reference many at the end of each chapter in this manual.

2. Develop a list of potential facilities with Alzheimer's units in your area. One very good resource is the Alzheimer's Association website (www.alz.org), where you can identify Alzheimer's Dementia nursing centers in your city and state. You can also use any good search engine.

3. Contact the Geriatric Program Director (described above) at each of these facilities and explain the program, then determine whether they are interested enough to meet with you. We recommend that you both send a letter (sample provided at end of this chapter) and follow up very quickly with a phone call to assess initial interest and schedule a meeting if appropriate.

   How to describe the program: *The program is a music/medical partnership designed to enhance cognitive abilities and improve behavior of people with middle to late stage Alzheimer's dementia. It works by providing diverse but consistent stimulation through frequent live musical performances at a time of day when many individuals are typically experiencing the most negative aspects of their ailment, i.e., "sundowning time," the late afternoon hours. Music reaches deeply into the minds of these people, especially during these vulnerable hours, and a Cognitive Behavior Modification through Music program can become a significant component of medical treatment, providing an upgrade in treatment and care that results in observable improvements in residents' quality of life. Morale also typically improves not only for the individuals directly involved in the project, but also amongst other residents who are able to attend the sessions, and among the staff responsible for caring for all participating residents.*

Major Steps, cont'd.

4. Send brief, general background materials to the Geriatric Program Director before your meeting, possibly including:
   - NCMC Final Report
   - Other articles or information that may have seemed especially informative or persuasive to you; we point to many different resources in this manual, and new articles and studies are being published quite often, so you may very find new materials that seem useful.

5. Meet with Geriatric Program Director, explain program & ascertain level of need and interest (Sample questions provided at end of this chapter)

6. Meet with other facility staff as listed in Key People section, explain program & ascertain level of need and interest

7. Using criteria listed above, determine whether to proceed with this facility or seek another partnering institution

8. Provide more in-depth background information about music and brain function to the Geriatric Program Director. These can include many of the books and articles already mentioned in the first two chapters of this manual.

9. Reach a formal, written agreement with the facility that details basic expectations and requirements for each party. A sample written agreement is provided at the end of this chapter.

10. After the facility and the music center have reached an agreement, the Geriatric Program Director will need to meet with other managers within the facility, including the Director of Nursing, the unit nursing manager, the Activities Director, the Food Manager (kitchen staff) and Head of Maintenance, in order to prepare for the program. The Music Center's Program Administrator should also be involved in these meetings in order to assure that everyone's expectations and responsibilities are clear and mutually agreed upon.

    A sample list of questions to be addressed during these meetings is provided at the end of this chapter.

Major Steps, cont'd.

The meetings with facility staff should include the following:

- Geriatric Program Director meets with facility Director of Nursing & unit Nursing Manager of 8 AM-4 PM shift to plan responsibilities and education for Certified Nursing Assistants. (Half of the staff will be from 7 AM to 3 PM shift, half will be on the 3PM to 11PM shift).

- Geriatric Program Director and Activities Director meet to outline budget (tuning piano, etc), scheduling at 3:30-4:30 time period, location considerations, and education for Activities Assistants.

- Geriatric Program Director meets with Food Service Manager to arrange scheduling.

- Geriatric Program Director and head of Maintenance meet to arrange for requirements such as air conditioning, helping musicians haul in instruments, special equipment needs, cords, etc.

11. Schedule and conduct orientation sessions for all facility staff who will be affected by (or who may affect) the program. Sample orientation materials are provided as an appendix to this manual. agreement is provided at the end of this chapter.

12. Schedule and conduct a few trial performances using experienced musicians to make sure everyone understands their responsibilities and commitments.

Cautions

The program will very often involve children coming from the Music Center with their teachers to perform. Children should be carefully prepared before arriving at the facility. For more information, see Chapter 5: Musicians.

The facility must provide a place on-site to secure equipment (microphone, amplifier/speaker, music stands, piano).

The Geriatric Program Director must make sure that all CNAs understand that residents need to be appropriately dressed and toileted before the performance.

Tips   A person must be available to greet all performers, teachers, and parents upon arrival at the facility to make sure they understand the value of their performance, the importance of being respectful, and make them feel welcome.

This individual should also guide performers to the performance space and explain that no one from the music center should be roaming the halls without permission and an escort from the facility.

The greeter may be either from the facility or from the music center; whoever it is, the message communicated to performers should be consistent.

Tools & Forms
- Performance room requirements
- Sample letter for initial contact with facilities
- Sample letter of agreement between music center and facility
- List of questions/questionnaire for facility staff

References   Alzheimer's Assocation: www.alz.org

Performance Room Requirements

Key Criteria   The performance room must meet the following basic requirements:
- A contained space, with no through traffic or other ongoing distractions, not a large auditorium.
- Audience space for at least 25-30 people, including residents, attendants, parents of young performers, etc.
- Ample room for the piano and multiple performers.
- Ample room for maneuvering wheelchairs and walkers.
- Easily accessible from the Alzheimer's unit.

Furniture & Fixtures   The following basic furniture should be provided:
- Tray tables for residents—provides space for drinks and snacks, musical instruments (if these are provided to audience members as part of a performance)
- Folding chairs for musicians
- Two music stands
- Electrical outlets near performers
- Lighting above piano and music stands
- Adjustable piano bench for wide range of performers (important)

Optional   Some people may want to stand and move or dance to the music. If feasible, and depending on the facility and the residents, you may also want to make sure that an open space is available within the room for dancing or movement.

Sample Letter for Initial Contact with Facilities

Purpose of this letter: To make initial contact with Geriatric Program Directors at facilities near the Community Music School and identify any interested. To be followed up within one week by telephone call to assess interest and schedule a meeting if appropriate.

Dear [GERIATRIC PROGRAM DIRECTOR],

How did you first learn the alphabet? Was it by singing the A-B-Cs? For many of us, the alphabet tune is a handy tool that pops into mind any time we sort items by letter. But what if music were the only way you could recall anything?

Oliver Sacks, in his book *Musicophilia*, describes a man with Alzheimer's Dementia who could complete the basic activities of daily living, such as getting dressed, only by singing himself through the steps.

If that works, is it possible that we can intentionally use music to help people whose connections with the external world have frayed to recover some of their own memories, or even to rebuild some cognitive abilities?

Based on research completed by Sacks, Daniel Levitin, and others, and on work done over two years in Massachusetts by the Northampton Community Music Center (NCMC) and the Northampton Rehabilitation and Nursing Center (NRNC), we believe that it is possible. The Northampton project, *Cognitive Behavior Modification Through Music*, showed remarkable results among a population of residents diagnosed with middle to late stage Alzheimer's dementia. And benefits were also discovered for facility staff, the families of residents, and the performers!

NCMC and NRNC have documented the results of their study, which was funded by the F.A.O. Schwarz Family Foundation, at www.ncmc.net/specialprojects.html. They have also developed a set of tools to help other Community Music Centers and Alzheimer's facilities launch similar programs. We would like to meet with you to discuss these ideas and tools further and to explore whether a similar partnership might work between our organizations.

Music can provide structure for thought, connections between people, and access to memories and feelings otherwise locked away. We will contact you soon to see whether you're interested in learning if and how our program might benefit your facility. We look forward to speaking with you.

Sincerely,
[COMMUNITY MUSIC CENTER EXECUTIVE DIRECTOR]

Sample Letter of Agreement

AGREEMENT

This document serves as an agreement between [MUSIC CENTER] and [NURSING CENTER], whereby students, teachers, and community members affiliated with [MUSIC CENTER] will conduct musical performances for the residents of the Alzheimer's Unit at [NURSING CENTER].

[MUSIC CENTER] will be responsible for scheduling all performances and alerting [NURSING CENTER] of all bookings and schedule changes as they occur. [MUSIC CENTER] will also manage all grants affiliated with the program and be responsible for supervising all monetary spending affiliated with the program.

[NURSING CENTER] will be responsible for providing appropriate space at its facility, making sure its staff adequately prepares and accompanies its residents for each musical performance. [NURSING CENTER] will also be responsible for keeping the piano, equipment, and all other materials acquired for this program safe from harm and theft, and in adequate working condition.

[MUSIC CENTER] will aim to provide 2-3 musical performances per week of approximately 45 minutes in length. This is, however, contingent upon available resources.

_____
Signature [MUSIC CENTER DIRECTOR]   Date

_____
Signature [NURSING CENTER DIRECTOR]   Date

Sample Questions for Geriatric Program Director

What musical activities do you now provide for your residents, or have you provided in the past? (e.g., music therapy, regular entertainment, holiday concerts, excursions, etc.)

Who has been responsible for coordinating your musical activities?

Have any of the musical activities been specifically addressed to people living with Alzheimer's?

What questions do you have about the *Cognitive Behavior Modification Through Music Program*?

Please describe for me how you see this program benefiting your facility.

Who on your facility's staff needs to be involved in making a decision on whether or not to implement this program?

If you decide to implement the program, who on your staff will be critical for helping us succeed?

In order for the program to have the most beneficial impact, we need to schedule most (if not all) of the performances during "sundowning" time, that is, between 3:00 PM and 4:30 PM. What space would you have available for performances during that time? What other activities might conflict during that time?

Also in order for the program to have the most beneficial impact, we need to have a minimum of two performances a week, with three being ideal. Would this be possible? Do you see any problems with that frequency?

Sample Questions for Geriatric Program Director

Would there be any problems with your various departments working together to help us run the program? The nursing staff, maintenance, food service, and housekeeping will probably all be affected, and there may be times when responsibilities need to be shared across departments. An example would be when the room needs to be set up for performances and then rearranged afterwards for dining; sometimes union rules might get in the way of accomplishing this setup quickly. Would something like that be a problem here?

It is important that unit CNAs and Aides understand their roles in this music-medical partnership, and we can help provide some orientation training for them. How would you schedule in-service training for them?

In order to launch the program right, we need to start with a smaller group of residents in the audience, then expand when we all have the logistics worked out. Who knows the residents best and would be able to help us select the initial group?

Communication will be very important during this program. How would you circulate the information on dates, performers, and instruments to your staff, so they can make sure that the room is ready and residents are prepared and arrive on time?

We also need to make sure we have consistent communication between you and the music center's representative, so that information on dates, performers, and so on is clear, and so that any problems can be addressed immediately. How would you like to see that communication structured?

Any direct costs to your facility for this program should be quite low. We would look for a basic financial commitment from you, however, in obtaining a piano to be dedicated to this program, and keeping it tuned. We also need to have a microphone and speaker and at least two music stands available for every performance. Would any of these costs be impossible for you?

What reservations or doubts do you have about the program?

How would you be able to tell that program is successful?

Chapter 4: Your Audience

Chapter Goals

Our goals in this chapter are to enable you to work with the Alzheimer's Facility staff to identify the residents who will be the best match for <u>launching</u> your Cognitive Behavior Modification through Music program and to help you and the staff prepare the residents and your performers for a successful program.

Objectives

The information and tools provided in this chapter will help you work with the Geriatric Program Director and Activities Director to:
- explain how and why the program will benefit participants, their caretakers, and the facility
- identify residents who will potentially benefit from a cognitive music program
- identify residents who may not benefit immediately, or who may disrupt performances
- select residents for participation in the initial program (for a phased implementation)
- explain to performers what reactions and results can be anticipated for the residents who participate

Introduction

In order for you to work most successfully with people living with Alzheimer's, a basic understanding of the disease afflicting them is very important. You should also be able to communicate this basic information to the teachers and students who will be performing, so that they can know what to expect and understand the reactions they will get before, during, and after performances. The following pages of this chapter provide some very brief information about the disease, including some terms and concepts that will certainly come up in your discussions with Alzheimer's facilities. Much more detail is available on the website of the Alzheimer's Association (www.alz.org) and in David Shenk's The Forgetting: Alzheimer's: Portrait of an Epidemic. We highly recommend that you consult both of these sources.

First, it's important to keep in mind that people suffering from Alzheimer's disease haven't disappeared, despite the problems they may have in communication and perception and even physical control. In testimony that Dr. Oliver Sacks provided to the U.S. Senate Special Committee on Aging in 1991, he made the point that "persons with Alzheimer's disease have not lost their memories nor their former personalities. They have lost access to them. For many people, the key to opening the locked door to the storehouse of long term memories and former personality is therapeutic use of the right music."

If there is one concept that you should keep in mind and communicate constantly while launching and running the program, it is this: *We must do our very best to see beyond the disease to the individuals trapped inside and use our music to help them reconnect.*

Who are they?

One way of seeing beyond the disease is to try and learn a little about each of the residents, especially those who make up your regular core audience. What did they work at in their lives? Who are they, where did they come from?

Our group included a ballet dancer, a cardiologist, a church organist and choir director, the son of a Baptist preacher, housewives, a factory worker, people who had large extended families who visited them regularly, people who had no visitors, people who had grown up with no music around the house, some who never finished high school, others with college degrees, and so on. They shared only the disease, their location, and, we came to see, solace in music. And sharing the experience of so many live performances brought them together, creating a real sense of belonging to a community.

We watched connections grow between these residents, who seemed quite individually isolated when the music program commenced. Some made a point of sitting next to each other at every performance, and even held hands during the music.

What is Alzheimer's Disease?

According to the Alzheimer's Association (www.alz.org), Alzheimer's disease is a brain disorder named for German physician Alois Alzheimer, who first described it in 1906. Alzheimer's destroys brain cells, causing memory loss and problems with thinking and behavior severe enough to affect work, lifelong hobbies or social life.

Alzheimer's is a progressive and fatal brain disease. Today it is the seventh-leading cause of death in the United States. It is the most common form of dementia, accounting for 50 to 70 percent of dementia cases. There is no current cure, though symptoms may be treated with drugs for a while.

As many as 5.3 million Americans are living with Alzheimer's disease and this number is expected to climb radically in the coming years. David Shenk, author of The Forgetting: Alzheimer's: Portrait of an Epidemic, says on his website (www.davidshenk.com), Senile dementia is as old as humanity…But because relatively few people lived to old age before the 20th century -- the average life expectancy in 1900 was in the 40s -- senility has never been a major social concern. Now, with life expectancy climbing toward 80 and ninety percent of today's babies expected to live past 65, senile dementia is fast reaching epidemic levels."

Shenk also says, "Over an average of eight years, Alzheimer's shuts down the functions of the brain, beginning with short-term memory, then shifting to language and basic thinking skills, and finally impairing mobility and basic life functions like swallowing and breathing. For those who do not die of an unrelated condition in the interim, Alzheimer's is always fatal." The Alzheimer's Association offers slightly different numbers, saying, "It is important to note that not everyone will experience the same symptoms or progress at the same rate. People with Alzheimer's die an average of four to six years after diagnosis, but the duration of the disease can vary from three to 20 years."

Alzheimer's disease is related to physical damage to the brain. Two abnormal structures called plaques and tangles are prime suspects in damaging and killing nerve cells. **Plaques** build up between nerve cells. **Tangles** form inside dying cells. Though most people develop some plaques and tangles as they age, those with Alzheimer's tend to develop far more. The plaques and tangles tend to form in a predictable pattern, beginning in areas important in learning and memory and then spreading to other regions. Scientists are not absolutely sure what role plaques and tangles play in Alzheimer's disease. Most experts believe they somehow block communication among nerve cells and disrupt activities that cells need to survive.

What are the stages of Alzheimer's disease?

You will often hear stages of Alzheimer's disease categorized as early-stage, mid-stage, and late-stage, or mild, moderate, moderately severe and severe. The scale most commonly used for evaluating the status of the disease in an individual outlines key symptoms characterizing seven stages ranging from unimpaired function to very severe cognitive decline. This framework is based on a system developed by Barry Reisberg, M.D., Clinical Director of the New York University School of Medicine's Silberstein Aging and Dementia Research Center, and is described in much more detail at www.alz.org. In our Northampton study, we identified people who were evaluated at 4-6 on the scale for our initial group of participants. Later in the project, we also provided some performances in a different format and at a different time of day for some residents with late-stage Alzheimer's (6 to 7 on the scale.)

What is sundowning or Sundown Syndrome?

Many people suffering from dementia experience especially pronounced symptoms of stress and anxiety in the late afternoon to early evening; these hours are quite often the very lowest point of their days, and they may become more disoriented, tired, or change their communication patterns, becoming more outspoken or even mute.

Several different factors may typically cause sundowning, including tiredness and circadian cycles (how our bodies and brains respond to the hour of the day and the amount of daylight visible). Some researchers have suggested that wandering behavior may have some roots in our far-distant past, when hunter-gatherers might have become anxious to get everything done before sundown. Others think residents may feel that it's the end of the work day and that they're supposed to be headed home and need to be elsewhere.

Sometimes the effects of sundowning may be aggravated by the pattern of shift changes at most facilities. As the day shift workers finish up, they are often focusing on paperwork and distributing medications. The evening shift normally begins by reviewing records and catching up on the status of residents, who may be left alone and without stimulation during this more vulnerable time.

By providing musical performances at sundowning time, you will be giving the participants much-needed stimulation and connection when they need it the most. The routine of regular performances and the music itself will help them settle.

Neuro-plasticity

One of the most exciting recent discoveries in neuroscience is that the human brain is highly changeable (i.e., plastic), possessing the ability not only to create new neurons, but also to modify networks of existing neurons to better cope with new circumstances. This means that our brains can continue to change and grow throughout our lives and that we can intentionally train our brains to maintain and regain mental fitness. Our brains can sometimes develop new pathways when old ones are damaged.

The implications of these discoveries for treating Alzheimer's disease are discussed in an article titled "Brain Plasticity and Alzheimer's Disease," available through the website of the Society for Neuroscience (www.sfn.org).

Briefly, this article states that a great deal of ongoing research points to the possibility of delaying the onset and progress of degenerative brain diseases through steps taken to maintain and even enhance brain plasticity. Key among these steps is a rich, stimulating environment. "Brain plasticity exercises may one day help Alzheimer's disease patients. These include demanding sensory, cognitive, and motor activities that reengage and strengthen the brain systems involved in learning. Such brain plasticity training has helped normal aging adults improve memory."

The concept of neuroplasticity has only gained widespread acceptance among scientists within the past twenty years or so, and a great deal of research into the basic science continues. Already some strategies, games, and tools, including computer software, are available for building brain fitness. For additional information, one very accessible overview of neuroplasticity and its implications is the book The Brain That Changes Itself, by Norman Doidge, M.D.

How can music help people with Alzheimer's Disease?

Over the course of our two year project in Northampton, we observed a range of positive changes in the mood, cognitive abilities, and behavior of the participants in our project. Several people who were isolated and virtually silent when we began became much more talkative, interested, happy, alert, and generally less isolated over the months of the project. Many sang along, remembering the words to songs, and responded to and engaged with the musicians. These changes were remarked upon by project staff, facility staff, family members, other residents, and many of the musicians who were repeat performers.

The writings of other researchers support our observations, and also point to benefits to physical health and sense of well-being as direct results of music therapy for this and other populations. Consider the following quotes.

"The aim of music therapy in people with dementia is far broader…it seeks to address the emotions, cognitive powers, thoughts, memories, the surviving "self" of the patient, to stimulate these and bring them to the fore. It aims to enrich and enlarge existence, to give freedom, stability, organization, and focus." Oliver Sacks, Musicophilia, Pg. 372.

"The very act of engaging one's mind in creative ways affects health directly via many mind/body connections. Our brains are deeply connected to our bodies via nerves, hormones, and the immune system. Anything that stimulates the brain, reduces stress, and promotes a more balanced emotional response will trigger positive changes in the body." Gene Cohen, The Mature Mind: The Positive Power of the Aging Brain, Pg. 176.

"There are no medications that can bring back the past, deepen relationships, increase quality of life, and nourish the heart, mind and soul, yet this is exactly what the therapeutic use of music can do." Joan Butterfield Whitcomb, The American Journal of Alzheimer's Care and Related Disorders & Research, November/December 1993.

And finally, from Oliver Sacks again: "Music is no luxury to [these patients], but a necessity, and can have a power beyond anything else to restore them to themselves, and to others, at least for a while." Musicophilia, Pg. 385.

Unlocking Memories & Emotions

Most of us possess a personal soundtrack tied to our past; a song we hear on the radio can unleash a rush of memory, an instant little movie where we feel again the sights and conversations and even the physical sensations of a particular experience or time in our lives—*it was hot the evening I heard that song, and there were thunderstorms around, and we were driving out to the lake...*

Many people with Alzheimer's disease retain their soundtracks as well as the rest of us. According to Oliver Sacks, "Musical perception, musical sensibility, musical emotion, and musical memory can survive long after other forms of memory have disappeared. Music of the right kind can serve to orient and anchor a patient when almost nothing else can." Musicophilia, Pg. 373.

In a similar vein, Daniel Levitin says, "As a musician, I'm reminded on a daily basis of the utterly ineffable, indescribable powers of music. I've also witnessed the healing power of music firsthand. In old people's homes and convalescent hospitals, when people have lost their memory due to Alzheimer's disease, stroke, or other degenerative brain trauma, music is one of the last things to go. Old people who are otherwise unable to remember the names of their spouse or children, or even what year it is, can be brought arrestingly back to focus by hearing the music of their youth." The World in Six Songs, Pg. 92.

When performing for people living with Alzheimer's, you will help them unlock their memories; of course not everyone has memories attached to the same songs. The age of residents varies considerably, as does the geography of their past, so the memories of different people will be activated by different songs.

Emotions, however, can often be activated for many people by a single song, even one they may not ever have heard before. We have observed this quite often, no more visibly than during repeated performances by a very gifted and empathic shakuhachi player. None of the participants in our group had any real experience with the Japanese bamboo flute in their musical histories, yet all responded to the music in very deep and peaceful and settling ways.

Improving Mood & Behavior

Another area of significant benefits that we observed from regular musical performances was in the mood and behavior of our regular audience members. For example, one woman whose prevailing affect was quite lethargic and unresponsive began to recognize her own name again, and gradually moved to a great deal of interaction with the other residents, staff, and musicians. Another woman initially resisted attending the performances and was very jittery and anxious about leaving the unit; when the regular schedule of performances was established, though, she calmed down considerably when in attendance and even though she kept her eyes closed, would answer questions when she was addressed.

Improving Mood & Behavior, cont'd.

Another man sat on the edge of his chair at the beginning of the program and early on tried to leave the room within the first ten minutes or so; he gradually settled, willing to stay longer and longer until he'd finally remain in place for entire performances.

Based on our observation and the reports of staff, these changes in behavior and mood often lasted well beyond the actual performances. Oliver Sacks has observed similar effects: "There can, however, be longer-term effects of music for people with dementia—improvements of mood, behavior, even cognitive function—which can persist for hours or days after they have been set off by music." Sacks, Musicophilia, Pg. 382.

From Isolation to Community

We found that our core group of participants developed a very strong team relationship amongst themselves, experiencing a common set of expectations for how performances would run, the behavior expected during performances, and the rewards and enjoyment to be derived. These relationships carried over beyond the sessions, changing not only the way the residents saw themselves and others in their group, but also the way others saw them. The small group results showed up in various areas; the members of the group were a particularly positive influence on the large group ward exercise program that the Activities Director led every day in the day room at 10 AM. Here the larger group of residents were tossing the ball, dancing, singing, strengthening social connections through conversation, etc.

"It is astonishing to see mute, isolated, confused individuals warm to music, recognize it as familiar, and start to sing… It is even more astonishing to see a dozen deeply demented people—all in worlds or nonworlds of their own, seemingly incapable of any coherent reactions, let alone interactions—and how they respond to the presence of a music therapist who begins to play music in front of them. There is a sudden attention: a dozen pairs of distracted eyes fasten on the player. Torpid patients become alert and aware; agitated ones grow calmer……One or two people, perhaps, start to sing along, others join them, and soon the entire group—many of them virtually speechless before—is singing together, as much as they are able. "Together" is a crucial term, for a sense of community takes hold, and these patients who seemed incorrigibly isolated by their disease and dementia are able, at least for a while, to recognize and bond with others." Oliver Sacks, Musicophilia, Pg. 380.

Small group success inspires everyone. It sparks staff interest and the urge to make these benefits available for all residents, offering a framework for upgrading care on the inside. This positive effect extends beyond the walls of the facility. Small group initial involvement made it possible for performers to build trust, interact, and reflect on the presentations. This provided a framework for growth on the outside as benefits in knowledge, understanding, and participation flowed back to the entire community.

Music and Physical Health

Yet another important benefit of regular live music performances for people living with Alzheimer's, especially at sundowning time, is the potential impact on physical health. Once again Daniel Levitin provides a very helpful overview of some of the recognized links between music and health:

"In just the past three or four years, an emerging body of evidence is pointing scientists in new directions...Listening to, and even more so singing or playing, music can alter brain chemistry associated with well-being, stress reduction, and immune system fortitude...Several recent studies show that levels of immunoglobin A, an important antibody that is needed for fighting colds, flus, and other infections of the mucous system, increased following various forms of music therapy. In another study, levels of melatonin, norepinephrine, and epinephrine increased during a four-week course of music therapy, and then returned to pretherapy levels after the music therapy ended. Melatonin (a naturally occurring hormone in the brain) helps to regulate the body's natural sleep/waking cycle and has been shown effective in treating seasonal affective disorder, a type of depression... Both norepinephrine and epinephrine affect alertness and arousal, and activate reward centers in the brain. Music listening also directly affects serotonin, the well-known neurotransmitter that is very closely associated with the regulation of mood...All this from a song." The World in Six Songs, Pg. 98-99

Music + Residents + Staff = New Vision

When we first launched our program in Northampton, the staff responsible for daily care of the residents was not entirely enthusiastic, to say the least. Part of this response was due to the fact that many of the caregivers had come from a temp agency, which meant new people needed to be educated about the program very often. In a very short while, however, as the changes in individual mood, behavior, and cognitive abilities became very apparent, attitudes quickly changed. The program was viewed much more positively, because improving the lives of the participants correspondingly improved the jobs of the staff; even more than that, though, the changes in the residents served almost to rehumanize them to the staff.

Oliver Sacks quotes Gretta Sculthorp, Australian music therapist: "One of the loveliest outcomes of my work is that nursing staff can suddenly see their charges in a whole new light, as people who have had a past, and not only a past but a past with joy and delight in it." Musicophilia, Pg. 381.

Criteria for Selecting Participants

We recommend beginning with a small core group of 7-10 residents in order to keep the project manageable during startup. The core group will be your pilot audience, who will help you establish all the practices and routines necessary to make the program run successfully. After the first 4 weeks, you will be able to expand the performances to a wider audience. In Northampton, we averaged about 35-40 people in our audience for each performance, including the core participants, other residents, staff, and family members.

- Residents who are evaluated at 4-6 on GDS scale; still have some cognition, able to participate
- For initial group, may want to select those with some history of involvement with music, for example, played an instrument when younger, sang in a choir, loved to go to concerts, etc.
- For initial group, don't include residents with extreme behavioral issues such as uncontrollable yelling, wandering, etc.
- Mix genders and age range
- Diverse backgrounds
- Either wheelchair-bound or ambulatory
- Depending on the facility's size and physical layout, you may want to select residents from different floors or areas, so that responsibility for preparing and accompanying residents does not fall on just a few CNAs.

Including People with End Stage Alzheimer's Dementia

Although end-stage Alzheimer's Dementia residents could not be brought to a regular sundowning scheduled performance, we found that often a single performer such as a singer, guitarist, harpist, flutist or other appropriate instrumentalist was free to perform in the morning, around 10:15 or 10:30 A M.

This is a time when maybe four or five residents in wheelchairs or on stretchers could be brought into a small room and placed in a semi-circle close to the performer. Once this group was gathered together, there was usually need for just one staff person.

Key People & Required Support

- Geriatric Program Director—Needs to make sure that the performance room is not double-booked and is set up as needed. Also needs to be involved with identifying the individuals who will most benefit and should participate in the program. The Geriatric Program Director should also be the point person responsible for protecting patient privacy and confidentiality.

- Activities Director—Typically schedules events for residents and maintains the calendar. Should be involved to make sure that other events on the calendar don't conflict with the music program (and vice versa.)

- Director of Nursing—Needs to make it part of CNAs' formal assignment that residents are up and prepared ahead of time and transported to the performance space for each session. These directives will typically funnel through the unit managers.

- Facility Administrator—You should make sure that the facility's administrator understands the program and how you're selecting people to participate. Make sure that the administrator acknowledges any potential issues around liability, confidentiality, patient privacy, and infection control and agrees with your plans to deal with these issues.

- Psychiatrist—You should inform/educate the facility's psychiatrist about the program. He or she may be interested in the concept and potential effects and could be a valuable supporter or even participant, especially if your program includes a formal study.

Steps   Use the following steps to select people to participate as core members of your audience.

1. Music School's Executive Director and Music Program Coordinator communicate criteria for selecting participants to Geriatric Program Director and Activities Director.

2. Geriatric Program Director examines resident histories and medical charts and makes preliminary selection of participants.

3. Geriatric Program Director contacts closest person to resident for permission to interview family members and friends for additional information about the resident's history if information in chart is lacking (sample questions attached at the end of this chapter).

4. Geriatric Program Director exchanges findings with ward nursing staff, who will present information specific to selected individuals, including clinical data on medication regimes, habits, likes, problems, etc., and discuss ways to make successful initial personal contact with the resident about the program.

5. Music School's Executive Director, Music Program Coordinator, and Geriatric Program Director meet to discuss final selection of initial participants.

6. Depending on the people selected, you may decide to invite them to participate after they have been screened. Some who might benefit may be reluctant if asked, though, or fearful of leaving the familiarity of their room or ward. In these cases, you can encourage them to attend by positioning the sessions as a special event. We found that this type of resistance quickly disappeared once the program was up and running and residents had attended a few sessions.

Cautions
- Selecting participants may require reviewing confidential records or other information. If so, make sure that you have received permission from the Geriatric Program Administrator, who will likely need to secure this permission from each resident's outside contact person.

- Be aware of any infection control issues, especially with bed-bound individuals. You don't want to expose people with compromised immune systems to any outside infections, nor do you want to expose the musicians, students, or parents to any infections.

- When selecting people to participate, you may want to review the range of behaviors exhibited by each; those individuals who show a combination of too many disruptive, destructive, or fearful behaviors should be very carefully considered for inclusion.

Tips
- Start off with a smaller group of listeners, perhaps for the first month or two, until you get the sessions running smoothly, then expand your audience.

- Be sure you inform everyone daily about what is going on, especially as you are initially planning the program and identifying residents to participate.

Tools & Forms
- Resident Musical History Questionnaire

References   Zeisel, John, I'M STILL HERE, Avery, 2009. (www.ImStillHere.org)

Resident Musical History Questions

These questions will be very useful for the Geriatric Program Director to use when identifying and screening people living with Alzheimer's for inclusion in the pilot phase of the program. The information for selected individuals should also be provided (without identifying information) to the Community Music School's Music Program Coordinator so that more specific musical guidelines can be developed and provided to the musicians.

1. Where did the person live (geographical area—country, state, city, rural, etc.) during his/her first twenty years of life?

2. What was the person's experience with music at home?

3. Did he/she play any musical instruments? If so, what instruments, how long, etc.

4. Did he/she sing in a chorus, choir, etc.? In church? If so, where, when, how long?

5. Did he/she serve in the Armed Forces? Any memories of USO performances, music related to service?

6. Did he/she listen to music as an adult? What kind of music? E.g., classical, opera, ragtime, Dixieland, big band, polka, country, etc.

7. What is his/her favorite song?

8. Who is her/his favorite singer or musical act?

9. What songs were on the jukebox/radio/phonograph when he/she was young, especially as a teenager?

Chapter 5: Musicians

Chapter Goals

Our goals in this chapter are to enable you to identify and select musicians to participate in your Cognitive Behavior Modification through Music program and to help you and the musicians prepare and conduct successful performances.

Objectives

The information and tools provided in this chapter will enable you, the Community Music School Executive Director and/or Music Program Coordinator, to

- identify and select musicians for participation in the initial (pilot) performances (for a phased implementation)
- communicate to musicians, students, and parents how to prepare for the performances
- communicate to musicians, students, and parents how to conduct their performances and what to expect during the performances
- identify which musicians are most well-received and effective
- expand your group of regular contributing performers when the program is up and running

Overview   Many of the benefits of a Cognitive Behavior Modification through Music program will come from presenting the audience with a diversity of musicians and styles of music. And of course you'll need many musicians in order to schedule performances three times a week over many months!

For example, more than 100 musicians performed in the Northampton program in several hundred performances over a two year period. These musicians included

- Solo performers—classical and jazz pianists, a shakuhachi player, a drummer, a violist, an Irish fiddler, individual Suzuki students, and others
- Singers with accompanist—from young teen vocal students to an adult jazz singer to a Juilliard trained vocalist
- A Cappella groups from local colleges
- Ensembles—a guitar and flute duo, a flute trio, a family trio of piano, cello, and violin, a group playing Peruvian instruments, and others

These musicians were music teachers and their students from the community music school, amateur ensembles, working professionals, and groups from local schools and colleges, and they provided a great variety of stimulation to the residents. As an equally important benefit, these performances built ties to a much wider community for the residents, the staff, and the musicians, many of whom have returned to perform again and again.

Let's explore how you can go about recruiting and preparing musicians to perform in the program.

Recruiting Musicians within the School

How can you identify musicians from within the school who would be willing to participate?
In many cases, the Executive Director and Director of Faculty will already know which teachers are amenable to performances in community-oriented settings, or those who are most interested in the healing or spiritual aspects of music. Those teachers will be the most likely candidates for your initial performances. A second group you should definitely target will be those teachers who you feel might be interested in exploring this type of performance experience if the opportunity is presented, and you may have a sense of who these teachers are. Most schools also have some teachers whose ability to commit their time is more limited, whether from other priorities and preferences or a busy teaching schedule elsewhere.

How can you know whether individual teachers and their students might be suitable performers for the program?
We suggest that you cast a wide net at the beginning, though; rather than limiting your options, communicate the opportunity to your entire faculty and let them self-select.

Broadening Your Network

How can you identify musicians from the community who would be willing to participate? Where can you look?
- Contacts through adult students at your school who participate in other musical activities outside the school
- Local musicians, amateur and professional, who are friends and associates of your existing faculty
- Music teachers, band & chorus directors from public schools
- Local charter schools, especially performing arts oriented
- Faculty at local colleges and universities
- Church choirs
- Vocal groups: a cappella, jazz divas, barbershop quartets
- Suggestions from local music stores
- Children with outside ensembles

How can you know whether they will be suitable performers for the program? You won't always be able to know ahead of time. Only the experience will tell in many cases, and your best option is simply to do your very best to prepare the musicians ahead of time by providing as much background as possible on the program and the audience.

Criteria for Including Musicians

We recommend that you not turn anyone away from performing if they volunteer, unless the nature of the music they offer won't work for this audience. (See the section titled *"What Might Not Work"* on the next page.)

If the music will work, everyone can be included; more passive or inexperienced or timid performers may require more assistance from the Music Program Coordinator or their teacher, but the performances can be a real learning opportunity for these individuals.

Compensation & Other Motivational Techniques

If you are able to secure grant funding for your program (and we strongly recommend securing even a small amount of funding to help launch your pilot), you may be able to budget a stipend for participating faculty members. As mentioned earlier, performances will take place during peak teaching hours, and in many cases they may be giving up income in order to participate. (This may not be true if they normally conduct group lessons and are able to bring their group to the facility to perform in lieu of a regularly scheduled lesson.)

Money will not always be available to compensate performers; even when it is, you should always emphasize the greater benefits of this program for the residents, the staff and facility, and the musicians themselves. Earlier chapters in this manual provide lots of detail about the benefits of the program for residents. For musicians, the key benefits to emphasize will be the opportunities the program offers them to use their music for the higher purposes of connection and healing, and the chance for themselves and their students to practice performing in front of a very appreciative audience.

Large Ensembles	What is the largest ensemble that works? It depends, of course, on the type of music and instruments and the skills of the performers. While an eight or ten member a capella group might work fine, an eight or ten member brass choir might be too much volume. The best rule of thumb is to keep the performances intimate, not to depend on too much highly amplified sound.
What Might Not Work?	We have seen several performances that have been less successful simply because of the tonal range of the instruments. For example, many participants may find continual low sounds to be unsettling, so groups of like instruments in the low register, such as an ensemble of string basses, won't be well-received.
	At the other end of the musical spectrum, instruments that play too much in higher registers, such as piccolo or the highest notes of the violin or trumpet, will cause another set of problems. Many residents will have hearing aids, and high, loud notes can be painful for them.
	Beyond those two extremes, we've found it best to stay away from music that is experimental or unstructured. Spirited songs are fine, but stay away from anything that might seem aggressive. The next chapter provides much more information on how to select music, including styles that work and some sample programs that worked successfully for us.
How Should Musicians Prepare?	Respect the audience by preparing as you would for any recital or performance. Take the performance seriously.
	Select the pieces to be played ahead of time.
	Prepare an introduction for the group and musicians, providing a little background on each musician and indicating who plays what part (if applies.)
	Organize the program order and learn a little background you can share about each piece.
	Practice the program, and memorize whatever music you can.
	Organize the sheet music ahead of time, in program order, and preferably in binders so the music doesn't fall off the stands.
	Treat the performance as something special by dressing appropriately. While this certainly doesn't mean gowns and tuxes (though go ahead if you've got them and want to go with that!), we suggest that the musicians wear clothes that are at least a little dressy. The audience will appreciate it, and the performers will feel that the event is a little more special, too.

Tips for successful perform- ances for people with Alzheimer's

In most important ways, performing for an audience of people living with Alzheimer's should be no different from performing for any small audience in an informal session. While musicians should always treat these performances seriously and be respectful to the audience, these are not recitals. Musicians should strive to be as relaxed and open as possible; stiff, formal performances won't make anyone comfortable, performer or audience.

Many musicians are more comfortable playing their instruments or singing than they are speaking to an audience. These sessions offer a wonderful opportunity for musicians to overcome their reluctance to speak. Engage with the audience—connect with them and they'll connect with you, and each other!

Encourage audience members to sing along if they know the words to anything you play.

Above all, don't condescend to this audience. Don't treat them like children. Speak with them as adults, introduce the pieces you're playing, provide a little background on each. Never make the mistake of assuming that Alzheimer's disease makes people unaware simply because they're non-verbal.

Whenever possible, don't use music stands. Play from memory if you can. When you do need to use stands, try to keep them as low as possible— minimize physical barriers between the musicians and the audience

Respond when the audience speaks to you. Making connections is one of the most important goals of these performances, and you will be surprised at some of the conversations you have.

Inhibitions against speaking out will be lower among some of your audience, so don't be startled if someone speaks while you're playing. Don't be surprised by what they might say, either; it could be positive or it could be negative, and they could repeat themselves. For example, one of us encountered an audience member who kept saying, "Oops, back to the drawing board!" quite loudly before, during, and after our first piece. When we finished, her caregiver wheeled her out of the room, and another of the residents explained, "She always says that about everything!"

On the other hand, another participant surprised the musicians when they invited the audience to sing along to a particular song and she asked, "In what key?" They gave her the key, and when she began to sing, she was indeed in tune and in the right key. Never underestimate your audience!

Above all: HAVE FUN, and your audience will also!

Key People & Required Support

From the Community Music School
- Executive Director
- Music Program Coordinator
- Director of Faculty
- Faculty
- Students & Parents

Steps

Use these steps to recruit musicians to perform.

1. The Executive Director should begin communicating about the program with musicians early and often, as we've described in previous chapters. Every one on one interaction with teachers should provide some opportunity to mention the program and build enthusiasm and participation.

2. Continue to communicate about the program in every staff meeting.

3. Make sure staff meeting minutes go out to all teachers and that updates about the program are included there.

4. Follow up with emails, thanking musicians for participating, updating all teachers on performances that have been completed or are upcoming, and encouraging individuals who may have expressed interest but haven't yet committed to performing.

5. Do everything possible to support the musicians who agree to perform. This is especially important before their first performance in the program. Provide them with all the information you can to help them select a program and prepare their students.

6. Finally, always make sure you acknowledge those who have participated, both individually and publicly (in staff meetings, for example).

Cautions
- Don't rule out any performers from appearing at least once unless you're quite certain that their style of music or instruments won't work with the program's audience.

- At the same time, don't limit the performers unnecessarily to one particular type of music that you believe will be familiar to the audience already. The program's success depends on variety (among other factors!) and the breadth of your audience's tastes and what they will enjoy will certainly surprise everyone concerned.

Tips
- Cast a wide net in your search for musicians to participate in the program. You'll need many dedicated performers to sustain the program over time.

- Do everything possible to prepare the musicians ahead of their performance, especially the first time out.

Tools & Forms
- Sample Letter to Teachers
- Guidelines for Performers (NOTE: The two page handout provided on pages 57-58 duplicates content provided earlier in this chapter. We have formatted pages 57-58 as a handout that you can copy and reuse if you wish.)
- Permission Slip (we recommend using your existing permission slip, modify as necessary)

Sample Letter to Teachers

Dear NCMC teachers:

Beginning Dec 10, NCMC will begin its **Music for Alzheimer's Patients Project** at the Northampton Rehabilitation & Nursing Center. The intent of this project is to bring a variety of musical experiences to these patients over a 20-week period between the hours of 3:30 and 5:00, a period of the day known as "sundowning," when people living with Alzheimer's experience a drop in cognitive responsiveness. Research has shown that engaging these individuals in music during this time may positively affect change in their behavior and brain function.

I'm asking all of you to consider bringing a group of your students (or even just yourselves) to do a short performance (30 mins or so) at the Nursing Center some weekday afternoon between Dec 10 and May 20. Teachers from NCMC will each receive a $50 stipend for their participation in this project. Please come see me so we can discuss what will work and what days and times are available.

It would be wonderful (but it is not necessary) to include at least one piece of music that might trigger memory for these audience members (for instance, well-known tunes from the 20's, 30's, 40's and 50's, songs from childhood like Twinkle and Go Tell Aunt Rhody, pieces that might be linked to events or holidays, etc.) With the holidays just around the corner, I would love to hear from some of you soon.

In some cases, transportation between NCMC and the Nursing Center can be provided. If you think that will be an issue for your students, let me know with some notice and we'll see what can be arranged. (For instance, if the Brass Ensemble regularly gets dropped off at NCMC on Thursdays at 3:30 for rehearsal, we could arrange on one day to have a van ready to pick them up and take them back and forth without inconveniencing their parents at all.) Students will need to bring their own music stands (if needed). Folding chairs will be provided on site, and there is a Knabe baby grand piano available to use.

More information about Alzheimer's and this project in particular are attached. Please ask parents of students under age 18 to sign a permission slip and return it to you (one is included in this packet for you to photocopy as needed). You should then submit all permission slips to me for my files. On the day of your performance, Pam Hamberg of the Nursing Center will give a brief orientation to the students about what Alzheimer's is and what behaviors they may witness, and you will be greeted by Beverly Pickering, Project Coordinator. Rest assured, the residents selected for this project pose no danger to anyone.

Thanks in advance for your cooperation. I look forward to hearing from you.

Jason Trotta
Executive Director

Musical Performances for People with Alzheimer's
Guidelines for Performers

What is the program?

The Cognitive Behavior Modification Program is a music/medical partnership designed to enhance cognitive abilities and improve behavior of people with middle to late stage Alzheimer's dementia. It works by providing diverse but consistent stimulation through frequent live musical performances at a time of day when many residents are typically experiencing the most negative aspects of their ailment, i.e., "sundowning time," the late afternoon hours. Music reaches deeply into the minds of these individuals, especially during these vulnerable hours, and a Cognitive Behavior Modification through Music program can become a significant component of medical treatment, providing an upgrade in treatment and care that results in observable improvements in quality of life. Morale also typically improves not only for the participants directly involved in the project, but also amongst other residents who are able to attend the sessions, and among the staff responsible for caring for these residents.

How should musicians prepare?

Respect the audience by preparing as you would for any recital or performance. Take the performance seriously.

Select the pieces to be played ahead of time.

Prepare an introduction for the group and musicians, providing a little background on each musician and indicating who plays what part (if applies.)

Organize the program order and learn a little background you can share about each piece.

Practice the program.

Memorize whatever music you can.

Organize the sheet music ahead of time, in program order, and preferably in binders so the music doesn't fall off the stands.

Treat the performance as something special by dressing appropriately. While this certainly doesn't mean gowns and tuxes (though go ahead if you've got them and want to go with that!), we suggest that the musicians wear clothes that are at least a little dressy. The audience will appreciate it, and the performers will feel that the event is a little more special, too.

Tips for successful perform-ances for people with Alzheimer's

In most important ways, performing for an audience of people with Alzheimer's should be no different from performing for any small audience in an informal session. While musicians should always treat these performances seriously and be respectful to the audience, these are not recitals. Musicians should strive to be as relaxed and open as possible; stiff, formal performances won't make anyone comfortable, performer or audience.

Many musicians are more comfortable playing their instruments or singing than they are speaking to an audience. These sessions offer a wonderful opportunity for musicians to overcome their reluctance to speak. Engage with the audience—connect with them and they'll connect with you, and each other!

Encourage audience members to sing along if they know the words to anything you play.

Above all, don't condescend to this audience. Don't treat them like children. Speak with them as adults, introduce the pieces you're playing, provide a little background on each. Never make the mistake of assuming that Alzheimer's disease makes people unaware simply because they're non-verbal.

Whenever possible, don't use music stands. Play from memory if you can. When you do need to use stands, try to keep them as low as possible—minimize physical barriers between the musicians and the audience

Respond when the audience speaks to you. Making connections is one of the most important goals of these performances, and you will be surprised at some of the conversations you have.

Inhibitions against speaking out will be lower among some of your audience, so don't be startled if someone speaks while you're playing. Don't be surprised by what they might say, either; it could be positive or it could be negative, and they could repeat themselves. For example, one of us encountered an audience member who kept saying, "Oops, back to the drawing board!" quite loudly before, during, and after our first piece. When we finished, her caregiver wheeled her out of the room, and another of the residents explained, "She always says that about everything!"

On the other hand, another participant surprised the musicians when they invited the audience to sing along to a particular song and she asked, "In what key?" They gave her the key, and when she began to sing, she was indeed in tune and in the right key. Never underestimate your audience!

Above all: HAVE FUN, and your audience will also!

Chapter 6: Music

Chapter Goals

Our goals in this chapter are to help musicians select and perform compositions most likely to result in successful performances for people with middle to late stage Alzheimer's.

Objectives

The information and tools provided in this chapter will enable
- the Music Program Coordinator to develop a standard musical program structure for use in framing all performances
- the Music Program Coordinator and participating musicians to identify musical compositions that will potentially benefit people with Alzheimer's who are participating in a cognitive music program
- musicians to construct programs for individual performances

Overview

Selecting the right music for an audience of people afflicted with Alzheimer's Dementia is an important process. It's also one that should not be all that difficult. Many, many different types of music will work. When establishing performance programs, you should strive for a balance between repetition and variety. By developing a set overall structure for the performances, including regular warm-up music as the audience is brought in and settled plus standard opening and closing sing-alongs, you will create a familiar situation where the residents can relax and be comfortable.

Overview, cont'd.

A set structure is important because audience members will be at different levels in terms of how alert and aware they are of their surroundings and the people and events around them, or they will simply display their awareness and comfort level (or fears and discomfort) differently. Some may be reluctant even to leave the safety of their rooms when the program begins; others may be confused about where they are or why they are there and might object verbally or attempt to leave. Hearing the regular warm-up and opening song will set expectations for many of them and open them up to hearing something new.

Within the context of the standard structure, you will then be free to include a range of different performers and music that will provide a variety of stimulation to help foster cognition and communication. This will also help engage some audience members who may become bored and begin to speak out or attempt to leave if every performance by every musician is identical.

After you have communicated to the musicians the guidelines in the previous chapter and the information in this chapter, we recommend that you leave the choice of compositions up to the performers. Most musicians will be sensitive to whether the pieces they are playing are connecting with this audience, and will adjust accordingly. If they don't, the Music Program Coordinator may choose to step in and guide the performance by suggesting other songs, or may help wrap up the performance a bit early.

To help with selecting music, this chapter includes some general criteria for selecting music, information for structuring programs, and some sample programs that were well-received by our mixed audiences in the Northampton program.

General Criteria for Selecting Music

- Above all, musicians should use their own approach. They should have an overall plan that reflects their personality, their instruments, and the music that they love to learn and perform.
- Musicians should select a mix of slow, mid-tempo, and faster pieces, as they would when performing for any general audience.
- When possible, include some pieces that reflect resident ethnicity. For example, if the audience includes many people from a Polish background, musicians might include some polkas, as they might also include some Latin rhythms for a Hispanic audience or Celtic melodies for an Irish audience, and so on.
- Perform gospel, jazz, traditional, blues, classical, rags, or light rock. Stay away from music that is too loud or too aggressive and distant from the residents' experience, such as loud heavy metal or rap that includes profanity.

General Criteria for Selecting Music, cont'd.

- Nursery rhymes or traditional children's songs are best performed by children, not adults. In the rare instances where an adult sang children's songs to people with Alzheimer's, we observed some audience members becoming quite impatient and even offended at the condescension they perceived.
- Many residents have ear sensitivities that can become painfully aroused by pieces laden with passages of very high notes on instruments such as violin or piccolo or flute.
- Mood can be affected, too, by a program that consists only of slow, sad songs or continuous very low doleful sounds, such as pieces performed solely on double bass or other very low register instruments.

Structuring a Program

It's important to have a standard overall structure for the performances, no matter who the musicians might be.

- Before every performance, have the same individual play a pre-program warm-up. In the Northampton project, this performer was always the Music Program Coordinator, who would begin playing at 3:15 for a 3:30 performance. Live music helps the middle to late Alzheimer's Dementia residents begin to focus as they are brought in and settled into their positions in the audience.
- Once the audience is in place, finish the warm up program.
- Introduce the performers
- Begin every program with the same opening song that the audience sings along with. Again, this familiar event will help the residents focus on why they are there and what is about to happen. We recommend asking the audience to select an opening song during the first performance or two. In Northampton, the audience selected *The Star Spangled Banner* and we began every performance by singing the national anthem with the Music Program Coordinator as accompanist.
- After the opening song, turn the performance over to the musicians.
- Remember, it is very important for musicians to engage the audience during the performance. They should speak to the residents as if they are concert goers, and introduce the members of the ensemble and announce at least the title of each piece. If they know some background about the piece, they should share their knowledge about the music. If any of the instruments are special or unusual, most of the audience will be interested in an explanation of the instruments.
- Attention spans of residents will be short, especially when performances are first begun, so musicians should structure their programs accordingly. When we began the Northampton program, the average attention span was 10-15 minutes maximum. This became longer over the course of many performances, eventually reaching a point where most or all of the group could remain engaged for as long as 45 minutes.
- Also because of short attention spans, each piece of music should be kept to no more than 3 to 4 minutes. Longer pieces will result in a more restless audience and will probably be counter-productive.

Structuring a Program, cont'd.

- When the musicians have completed their program, the Music Program Coordinator should step in and thank them, possibly introduce them again, and lead the applause.
- The Music Program Coordinator (or other regular player) should then lead a standard closing song. In Northampton, our audience and the Program Director selected *Till We Meet Again* and we closed every performance by singing this song with the Program Director as accompanist.

Key People & Required Support

The Music Program Coordinator is responsible for establishing the overall structure for the performances, running the sessions according to that structure, and communicating with the music teachers and other musicians about their selection of compositions to perform.

Music Teachers & Musicians are responsible for selecting and preparing pieces that fall within the guidelines. They should learn something about the background of the pieces so they can explain them to the audience. During performances, the musicians should pay close attention to what compositions are engaging the audience, which ones are not, and make note of this for the development of future performance programs.

Steps

The Music Program Coordinator, with assistance from an intern if available, should

1. Identify music to be used for the pre-program warm-up
2. Establish an overall structure for the performances, including warm-up music, an opening song, and a closing song. Whenever possible, select the opening and closing sing-alongs with the participation of the audience members early on in the program.
3. Provide guidelines to the musicians before their performances, so they know what pieces to prepare and how to conduct their performances. (We recommend simply copying the previous chapter and this one and providing them to the musicians.)
4. Especially in the first months of the programs, stick to the format: warm-up music as audience enters, opening sing-along, performance by musicians, closing sing-along.
5. Provide feedback to the musicians immediately after every performance about the music they selected, including what worked and why, and what didn't. Make sure you also solicit their feedback on what they felt worked and didn't. Document these observations. (More information and forms for documenting are provided in the next chapter, Running the Sessions.)
6. Solicit feedback from the staff and audience about what music was successful and what wasn't. (Again, more information and forms for this are provided in the next chapter, Running the Sessions.)

Cautions   Be aware in advance of performers' plans, including the type of music, number of performers in a group, instruments, and general volume level so you can steer away from potential problems.

Tips   Use the tools and structures we provide throughout this manual, including the sample programs at the end of this chapter, to help guide your efforts. We're certainly not saying that we know the only way to launch and run this program, but we've learned some lessons that will benefit you.

The Music Program Coordinator should always be prepared to help out or intervene during performances if the musicians are having problems connecting with the audience. The next chapter provides some more ideas on how to do so.

Tools & Forms   Sample programs (following pages)

References   If musicians have any difficulty finding background on their selections, direct them to standard web-based resources such as Wikipedia, which provides information on a surprising number of musicians and compositions.

Sample Programs   The following pages include some sample programs that can be used for assistance in identifying specific compositions that may work for your audience. The sample programs also demonstrate how widely varied the musical offerings can be within the context of a standard program.

These sample programs represent a cross-section of the musicians who have contributed to the Northampton project; many others have also joined in. Use these programs as models for your own, picking whatever tunes work for your taste, style, and instruments.

Warm-up Pieces   All from one book! *PIANO CLASSICS, 90 TIMELESS PIECES FROM THE MASTERS*, Sterling Publishers, New York/London

Prelude No.1 from the Well-Tempered Clavier	Johann Sebastian Bach
Für Elise	Ludwig van Beethoven
Mazurka in B Flat, Op. 7, No. 1	Frederic Chopin
Clair de Lune	Claude Debussy
Valse, Op. 64, No. 2	Frederic Chopin
The Cascades	Scott Joplin
Sonata, K. 545, Allegro	Wolfgang Amadeus Mozart

Unaccompa-nied Female Vocalist

An interactive program performed multiple times for an audience of people with mid-stage to late-stage Alzheimer's. This singer performed very often, and encouraged audience members to sing along. She believed that repetition of the same program in every one of her appearances would provide continuity and learning for the audience, and she was right. Some who barely reacted at first were singing along, or mouthing the words, after numerous hearings.

Star Spangled Banner	*Francis Scott Key*
This Little Light of Mine	Henry Dixon Loes
Glory, Hallelujah	William Steffe
This Train Is Bound For Glory	Woody Guthrie
You Are My Sunshine	Governor Jimmie Davies & Charles Mitchell
Fly Me To The Moon	Bart Howard
Moon River	Henry Mancini & Johnny Mercer
By The Light Of The Silvery Moon	Gus Edwards & Edward Madden
Everything's Gonna Be Alright	Michael Brooks
Down By the Riverside	African American Spiritual
Till We Meet Again	*Richard Whiting & Raymond Egan*

Unaccompanied Female Vocalist

This is a program used by the same vocalist as the program above; she sang these songs in a separate series of regular performances (often weekly) for a smaller group of late-stage Alzheimer's patients only. These individuals were non-communicative, and she sang to them without expecting them to sing along. Their response over time was much greater than anyone anticipated.

Star Spangled Banner	*Francis Scott Key*
In The Morning	Sweet Honey In The Rock
Wade In The Water	Thomas A. Dorsey
I'll Fly Away	Albert E. Brumley
When The Storms of Life Are Raging	Charles A. Tindley
This Little Light Of Mine	Harry Dixon Loes
This Train Is Bound For Glory	Woody Guthrie
Glory, Hallelujah	William Steffe
O Holy Night	Adolphe Charles Adam
Go Tell It On The Mountain	Frederick Jerome Work
Silent Night	Franz Xaver Gruber
You Are My Sunshine	Governor Jimmie Davies & Charles Mitchell
Till We Meet Again	*Richard Whiting & Raymond Egan*

Family String Trio Program

Program performed by a family string trio, consisting of mother on cello, son, age 9, on piano, and daughter, age 5, on violin. This was the longest performing session of any, more than 45 minutes in length. Because it occurred in the second year of our program, the audience stayed engaged for the entire concert, something that most would not have been able to do earlier in the program.

Star Spangled Banner	*Francis Scott key*
Allegro	S. Suzuki
Go Tell Aunt Rhody	Traditional American
Lightly Row	Traditional German
Twinkle Twinkle	Wolfgang Amadeus Mozart
May Song	Unknown
Long Long Ago	Thomas Haynes Bayly
Arietta	Wolfgang Amadeus Mozart
Allegro	S. Suzuki
Melody	Robert Schumann
Cradle Song	Charles Maria von Weber
Suite for solo cello in G	Johann Sebastian Bach
(Prelude, Allemande, Courante, Sarabande, Minuets I & II, Gigue)	
Salut d'amour, Op. 12	Edward Elgar
The Train Whistle (from 10 American Cello Etudes)	Aaron Minsky
Arioso	Johann Sebastian Bach
Till We Meet Again	*Richard Whiting & Raymond Egan*

Flute Trio   Pieces used various combinations of concert, alto, and bass flutes

Star Spangled Banner	*Francis Scott Key*
Fantasie I	Edward Blanke
Fantasie VI	Edward Blanke
Trio Sonata (Largo & Allegro)	Johann Sebastian Bach
Trio, Op. 83, No. 2 Allegretto)	James Hook
Trio, Op. 83, No.3, (Rondo)	James Hook
Asa Branca	Luis Gonzaga e Humberto Teixeira
Brandenburg Concerto No. 5 (Allegro)	Johann Sebastian Bach
Blue Moon	Herschel Burke Gilbert
Let Me Call You Sweetheart	Leo Friedman & Beth Slater Whitson
Till We Meet Again	*Richard Whiting & Raymond Egan*

Unaccompanied Viola

Star Spangled Banner	*Francis Scott Key*
America The Beautiful	Samuel A. Ward & Katherine Lee Bates
Cello Suite No. 1 Prelude, Courante, Gavotte	J.S. Bach
Yesterday	John Lennon & Paul McCartney
When I'm Sixty Four	Paul McCartney
Hungarian Rhapsody	Johannes Brahms
Ashokan Farewell	Jay Ungar
The Little Red Lark	Irish Traditional
Shrewsbury Lasses	Traditional English Dance
Till We Meet Again	*Richard Whiting & Raymond Egan*

Shakuhachi Flute

Listening, breathing, imagining, following sound patterns. Listeners were quite entranced by this music, and the performer was very moved also. She has appeared many times, each time with a somewhat different program. She begins each performance with an explanation of the five tones of the shakuhachi, and plays a warm-up exercise. Some of the participants have begun to hum along with each tone as she plays. She often organizes her programs around a theme, such as Springtime or the long light at the summer solstice. This program is an example of only one of her appearances.

Star Spangled Banner	*Francis Scott Key*
Toning = 5 body energy centers = 5 tones from lowest to highest	
Ajikan: Breathing together	Traditional Japanese
Kurokami: Sounds flowing through the 5 energy centers	Traditional Japanese
Koi De: Black hair becoming white	Traditional Japanese
Haru No Umi (The Sea in Springtime)	Michio Miyagi
Amazing Grace	John Newton
Till We Meet Again	*Richard Whiting & Raymond Egan*

Percussion-ist With Hand Drums

The percussionist brought many different drums and percussion instruments, such as shakers, xylophone, etc., and distributed them throughout the audience. These sessions were the most interactive of all, and were surprisingly successful. Although many residents could not remember the names of the percussion instruments from one performance to the next (often monthly in this case), the performer says that she could see many of them remembering how to PLAY the instruments from one session to the next, and improving their abilities.

Star Spangled Banner	*Francis Scott Key*
Improvisation Solo	
Improvisation with group: pass out instruments- introduce beat structure	
Improvisation with group: everyone participates to create own rhythm	
Improvisation with group: build rhythmic patterns on body responses to inner feelings	
Till We Meet Again	*Richard Whiting & Raymond Egan*

Voice Teacher & Students

A voice teacher brought seven of her high school age vocal students to perform; the teacher was the accompanist, and each of the students performed one or more songs as a solo. This program was all solo singers with piano; the students did not sing as a group. The students were quite popular with the residents.

Star Spangled Banner	*Francis Scott Key*
Giants In The Sky	Stephen Sondheim
Ten Minutes Ago	Richard Rodgers & Oscar Hammerstein
My Funny Valentine	Richard Rodgers & Lorenz Hart
I've Got The Sun In The Morning	Irving Berlin
Don't Take Your Love Away From Me	Connell Moss & Randy Travis
So In Love	Cole Porter
Una Donna A Quindici Anni	Wolfgang Amadeus Mozart
The Dodger (Folk Song)	Aaron Copland
Perhaps, Perhaps, Perhaps	Composer Unknown
Feeling Groovy	Paul Simon
It's Only A Paper Moon	Harold Arlen & E. Y. "Yip" Harburg
So In Love	Cole Porter
The Lonely Goatherd	Richard Rodgers & Oscar Hammerstein
Lachen Und Weinen	Franz Peter Schubert
Poor Wandering One	Arthur Sullivan
I Could Have Danced All Night	Alan J. Lerner & Frederick Loewe
Till We Meet Again	*Richard Whiting & Raymond Egan*

Berkshire Hills Music Academy

The Berkshire Hills Music Academy, in South Hadley, Massachusetts, is a private post-secondary residential school that provides young adults with developmental or learning disabilities the opportunity to cultivate their musical talents. Berkshire Hills has brought groups to perform on various instruments and in various groupings, including piano, vocals, harmonica, guitar, pan pipes, flute, shakers, etc. Below are listings for a couple of sample programs presented by this organization.

Star Spangled Banner	*Francis Scott Key*
Hey Good Lookin' (Trio)	Hank Williams
Blowin' In The Wind (Guitar, Harmonica, Vocals)	Bob Dylan
Red River Valley	Traditional
Home On The Range	David Guion
If I Had A Hammer	Pete Segar & Lee Hays
You Are My Sunshine	Governor Jimmie Davies
Will The Circle Be Unbroken	Charles Gabriel
Pituco (Panpipes, Flute, Shakers)	Peruvian Composer
Phunuruhas	Peruvian
Chacharpayadelindio	Peruvian
Ain't Misbehavin	Fats Waller &Thomas Wright
All of Me	Gerald Marks
Crazy Over You	Rodney Foster & Bill Lloyd
What A Wonderful World	Bob Thiele & George David Weiss
Twist And Shout (Trio)	Lennon/McCartney
Till We Meet Again	*Richard Whiting & Raymond Egan*

More Berkshire Hills Music Academy Songs

Put On A Happy Face	Charles Strause & Lee Adams
Cheating On You	Franz Ferdinand
Nova Scotia	Traditional
Georgia On My Mind	Hoagy Carmichael
Summertime	George Gershwin
Can't Help Falling In Love	Elvis Presley
Let it Be	John Lennon
O Mio Babbino Caro	Giacomo Puccini
Deed I Do	Shepard N. Edmonds
Yesterday	John Lennon & Paul McCartney
Hello, Dolly	Jerry Herman

**Violinist/
Teacher &
Shin'ichi
Suzuki
Violin
Students**

A Suzuki violin teacher brought her groups of students multiple times; these children ranged in age from 4-12.

Star Spangled Banner	*Francis Scott Key*
Twinkle Twinkle Little Star Variations	Wolfgang Amadeus Mozart, (S. Suzuki arr.)
Lightly Row	Folk Song
Song of the Wind	Folk song
Go Tell Aunt Rhody	Folk Song
O Come, Little Children	Folk song
May Song	Folk Song
Long Long Ago	Thomas Haynes Bayly
Allegro	S. Suzuki
Andantino	S. Suzuki
Minuet 1	J.S. Bach
Minuet 2	J.S. Bach
Minuet 3	J.S. Bach
Gavotte	Francois Joseph Gossec
Chorus from Judas Maccabeus	George Frederick Handel
Hunter's Chorus	Carl Maria von Weber
Allegretto	S. Suzuki
Perpetual Motion	S. Suzuki
Till We Meet Again	*Richard Whiting & Raymond Egan*

Amherst College A Cappella Group: "Sabrinas"

This was one of several a cappella groups that appeared several times. All of these groups came from local colleges, and all were very well received.

Star Spangled Banner	*Francis Scott Key*
Show Me Love	Robyn
Love Fool	The Cardigans
Hear Me Out	Frou Frou
Hotel Song	Regina Spektor
Afternoon Delight	Starland Vocal Band
80's Medley:	
Like a Prayer	Madonna
Tainted Love	Soft Cell
Sweet Dreams (Are Made Of This)	Eurythmics
Helplessly Hoping	Crosby Stills Nash Young
Bring It On Home To Me	Sam Cooke
Lean On Me	Bill Withers
Till We Meet Again	*Richard Whiting & Raymond Egan*

Solo Jazz Piano

Star Spangled Banner	*Francis Scott key*
But Beautiful	Nat King Cole
Don't Blame Me	Jimmy McHugh
My Romance	Carly Simon
Darn That Dream	Jimmy Van Heusen/Eddie DeLange
Easy to Love	Cole Porter
In A Sentimental Mood	Duke Ellington
Improvisation	Stephen Page
Till We Meet Again	*Richard Whiting & Raymond Egan*

Chapter 7: Running the Sessions

Chapter Goals

Our goals in this chapter are to enable the Music Program Coordinator to plan and facilitate each performance day's activities in a manner that fosters good relationships with the facility staff and ensures the overall success of the program.

Objectives

The information and tools provided in this chapter will help the Music Program Coordinator work with the Alzheimer's facility staff, the musicians, and the audience to:

- Plan and schedule the music sessions
- Communicate the schedule to all who will be affected
- Prepare for each day's music session
- Conduct the sessions
- Wrap up each music session

Overview

Planning, scheduling, and running the frequent live music performances that are the heart of this program will require a very well-coordinated team effort. Constant communication will be necessary between the Music Coordinator and musicians; between the Music Coordinator and the Geriatric Program Director and Activities Director and Assistants; between the Geriatric Program Director and CNAs, administration, and other staff; and so on.

It will be important for the overall success of your program that every individual session runs well. Remember, though, as you have read in the chapters about musicians and music, that there should be room for experimentation in session content. You should expect some sessions to run better or be better received than others. As long as you maintain a standard structure and stick to the general guidelines about choices of music, both of which are described in Chapter 6, the residents will appreciate and benefit from the performances. In fact, offering a wider variety of music and occasionally challenging the audience will only make the program more interesting and more effective for everyone involved.

This chapter provides a detailed set of charts that break out the recommended tasks and responsibilities involved in planning and scheduling, setting up, running, and concluding music sessions. Before we go to the detail, though, let's discuss some critical considerations related to each phase.

Your Backup Plan (Very Important!)

People sometimes get their schedules mixed up, cars break down, family emergencies arise, and you may find yourself without a musician on the day of a scheduled session. Rather than canceling at the last minute, we recommend that the Music Coordinator (and intern, if you're lucky enough to have one!) always be prepared with a standard backup program that can be performed on little notice.

Your backup program may also be the same program you use to fill in on weeks when you're unable to schedule enough outside performers to provide the minimum number of 2 to 3 performances at sundowning time. Maintaining that frequency is essential to the effectiveness of the program, so your backup program should get a regular workout. Develop your own standard backup based on the repertoire you are most comfortable with and the music you have observed working well with your audience.

Planning & Scheduling Sessions

Planning and scheduling the sessions, especially at the beginning of the program, will largely be the responsibility of the Community Music School Executive Director and the Music Program Coordinator. This will be when you identify the first group of teachers and performers who will be involved in the project's pilot sessions and subsequent performers.

Most importantly, this time is also when you should establish very clear communication channels and expectations for everyone who will be involved in your program. **Communication is critical!** You will find very quickly that your program involves many people; within the facility alone, you will interact with and depend upon CNAs, administrators, medical staff, the activities director and assistants, possibly social workers, an in-house music therapist who serves all residents within the facility, and others.

One of your most important tools for establishing communications and expectations will be the orientation/training session about the program that is delivered to staff before the program begins. Because some facilities have high turnover, especially amongst CNAs, you may need to hold regular refresher sessions of this orientation also, perhaps quarterly or annually (depending on turnover rates). Maintaining regular communications will be equally important, which means you should be providing updates to staff every time a music session is to be held.

Over the course of the program, you'll also be dealing with dozens of music teachers, students, their parents, and other volunteer musicians from the community. You may also need to schedule around other volunteers who provide entertainment or activities at the facility outside your structured program, including musicians, art therapists, dance or exercise instructors, and so on. Your program will also likely generate some local interest and you may be interacting with local press, radio, and TV.

Without clearly established communication channels and responsibilities, and without clear expectations for everyone from the beginning, your job as Music Program Coordinator or Executive Director will be much more difficult. The odds of running a successful long-term program will also be much lower without these prerequisites.

We recommend that you use the charts which appear at the end of this chapter as a guide to structure your activities and communications. Add any tasks you need to, skip any that don't apply, and alter the title of the individual responsible if necessary.

Before the Session

Each performance day, the Music Program Coordinator and the facility's point person for the project (normally the Geriatric Program Director or Activities Director) need to perform a standard set of tasks to make sure everything runs smoothly. The cooperation and support of all facility staff will be essential each time, and only good leadership and clear communication from the program principals will ensure the necessary level of collaboration.

The first broad set of responsibilities will be to communicate with staff early on the morning of each performance day, reminding them about the music session that day, what will be required, and when. Staff will usually need to be reminded again at afternoon shift change, when responsibilities will overlap or change from one person to another.

Next, the performance space will need to be readied in the afternoon. In most facilities, the room will have multiple uses, whether it doubles as a dining area or is used for exercise, games, crafts, or other activities. Exactly what needs to be done by the Music Program Coordinator and intern to set up the space will of course depend on the specific facility. At minimum you will probably need to retrieve the musical equipment, such as microphone and amplifier, music stands, extension cord, etc., from safe storage and set it up, and you may need to move the piano away from the wall and so on.

Tables and chairs for the audience will also need to be moved into the desired arrangement. When setting up chairs, we recommend saving a semi-circular area directly in front of the performers for your core group of participants, who you will have identified through the steps described in Chapter 4 of this manual. Normally this will mean leaving open space for wheelchairs along with some chairs; some of these audience members may also need small tables in front of them on which they can rest their hands, tap or drum, or place percussion instruments if the session uses them.

The Music Program Coordinator and/or intern will also be responsible for greeting the musicians and parents and helping them find the performance space and set up and store their belongings out of the way. This is when you should also make sure that all the performers have been briefed on what to expect, such as possible disruptions while they are playing from intercom announcements, attendants arriving to give residents medications or take them away to an appointment, restraint alarms on wheelchairs, and similar events. Point out the hand sanitizer and emphasize the importance of its use. Show the performers where you have provided water for them and warn them to keep it away from the piano. You should also make sure that the program for the day matches whatever has been communicated to you ahead of time and verify any information that you need for introducing the performers and beginning the session.

Preparing & Moving Residents

The music performances should always be treated as special events, as real concerts! Treating the performances as special events will be an important factor in building enthusiasm amongst residents and caregivers and will contribute significantly to overall improvements in morale and behavior.

Residents should always be prepared for the session before they leave their rooms. They should be woken from naps long enough before performance time that they can be as alert as possible. They should also be cleaned up as needed and toileted ahead of time. They should be dressed and have their hair combed or brushed. We have seen some residents become upset when they were moved to a performance without feeling presentable in public, so you need to be sensitive to their needs. One woman, for example, grew quite distraught at the thought of leaving her room without her wig in place.

Most of the audience for your music sessions will not be mobile on their own. Some may be confined to wheelchairs; at minimum, those who walk will usually need to be escorted from their rooms or ward because they will not be free to wander through the facility on their own.

Initially you may find some resistance to the necessary level of preparation among the staff responsible for completing it, as we did; they may perceive the sessions as only adding to their workload. You will need to use your best communication skills early on; after the program begins and participant behavior and mood start to improve, you will be able to (and should!) point out frequently how the changes benefit the residents and the staff who care for them.

Opening the Session
As we recommended in Chapter 6, a standard structure for beginning every music session is desirable, because it will provide the residents with a familiar sequence of events that will comfort and ground them. If you are recording your sessions, turn on the recorder before you begin, so you capture the introductions and can identify the musicians on the recording more easily later. The key components of this opening structure should be the following:

1. Introductory music as audience is brought into the room, played by Music Coordinator and/or intern. Recorded music might also be used, especially if an intern is not available to assist in greeting the musicians, but live music will be preferable.

2. Standard opening statement about the program, acknowledging the funder, and a reminder to the audience that they play an important role and should encourage the performers by singing along or clapping.

3. An introduction of the performers, including name of the leader and where they are from

4. Your standard opening composition (our audience selected *The Star Spangled Banner*)

During the Session

Once the Music Program Coordinator has introduced the group leader or music teacher, that individual should run the program. Typically the group leader introduces the students or other musicians, and will introduce each composition before it is played. Sessions usually work best when the group leader engages the audience by providing some interesting background about the piece, the composer, the instrument, etc.

If students are soloing as part of the performance, have them use the microphone and introduce themselves and the piece they are about to play. If students fail to do so, the Music Program Coordinator should feel free to ask them to do so before they begin playing, or at the end of the piece if necessary. Remember, an important component of the program is to provide educational benefits and performing experience for the students!

Audience members should be monitored during the performance for signs of restlessness, agitation, shouting, or other potentially disruptive behaviors, such as an inclination to get up and leave the room, physical discomfort, incontinence issues, etc. Often an alert staff member can spot developing problems early enough to sit with the individual and head the behaviors off or quietly remove the person from the room if needed.

The Music Program Coordinator should monitor the overall audience throughout the performance for restlessness, wandering attention, etc., and quietly ask the music group leader to shorten the program if necessary. (The music group leader should always be alerted ahead of time that this may be necessary.) The likelihood of needing to shorten the session will be greater near the beginning of your program, when your audience's attention span will be shortest. We found that our group's common attention span grew from about 10-15 minutes at the beginning of the Northampton program to a full 45 minutes by the second year of performances.

If a formal study is a component of your program, as we describe in a later chapter, you will also have standard observation forms that you use to capture the responses and behaviors of individual participants. These should be filled in by the Music Program Coordinator and intern <u>while</u> the performance is ongoing. You will find more information about this process and the forms in *Chapter 9: Documenting Your Program.*

Concluding the Session

Again as we recommended in Chapter 6, a standard structure for concluding every music session is desirable, because it will provide the residents with a familiar sequence of events that will comfort and ground them. The key components of the concluding structure should be the following:

1. After the last piece, thank the performers and mention their names again and lead a final round of applause.

2. If the program was short and the audience still seems engaged, you may want to play some additional sing-alongs, etc., to fill the remaining time

3. Give a standard concluding statement about the program, thanking the performers and their parents (if applies), the staff, and the audience.

4. Play your standard closing compositions (We use *Amazing Grace* and *Till We Meet Again*, and we distribute a sheet with the lyrics of the first of each immediately before singing the songs)

After the Session

The Music Program Coordinator's job does not end when the music stops. In order to maintain the best possible relations with facility staff, music teachers, and performers, and to continually adjust and improve the program, you should always complete the following steps:

Distribute feedback questionnaires to the music teacher or group leader (Sample provided at the end of this chapter.)

Provide feedback to the musicians about their program. Of course you'll generally want to keep this mostly positive, since the musicians will be volunteering their time. Point out what worked well. But if you saw compositions or behaviors that weren't beneficial for your audience, you may want to point them out, especially if the group seems interested in performing again and you want them to do so.

If possible, also allow time for the musicians and audience to interact. Given multiple uses of the room and the schedule at your facility, this may not be feasible. We have had teachers suggest this, though, as a way for their young students to connect more with the elderly audience. Interaction will certainly foster the community-building that is an intentional component of this program.

You may also want to play music as the residents are removed from the performance space to return to their ward or rooms. Performing live music during this time is highly preferable but may be difficult, because the Music Coordinator will have multiple responsibilities dealing with the residents and musicians and assuring that the musical equipment is secured. Recorded music may be very helpful at this time, depending on the quality of the facility's CD collection and audio equipment.

After the Session, cont'd.

Finally, leave the room in the best condition possible for the next scheduled activity. Usually the activities or maintenance staff will already be moving chairs and tables as you talk to the musicians and pack up and store all the musical equipment and move the piano back against wall if necessary. You can help assure good relations and attitude, though, by cleaning up water glasses, assisting if needed in returning tables and chairs to the required configuration, and so on.

Key People & Required Support

The charts at the end of this chapter provide more detail on running the sessions. Don't take these lists as being completely prescriptive. We provide them for you to use as a model that you can modify or select from as fits your specific situation. Because both Community Music Schools and Alzheimer's facilities can vary so widely in their size, staffing, and physical structure, the tasks and who completes them will probably vary correspondingly. What we present here is what worked for us in our situation, or, in some cases, reflects how we would do things now based on what we have learned.

Cautions If the session is not going well, intervene if necessary! If you must do so, though, do it gently, without offending the musicians or upsetting your audience. You might suggest that the musicians skip further ahead in their program if you spot compositions that aren't working or otherwise shorten the program.

If musicians don't show, be prepared to substitute! Don't cancel the performance at the last minute, because you will find that residents quickly grow to look forward to the sessions, and benefits to them are maximized by maintaining a regular schedule.

Protect the piano, the musican equipment, and the musicians' instruments. Performance spaces can often be crowded. It's very important to make sure that bottles and glasses of liquids not be placed on the piano or the equipment.

Tips Plan! Communicate constantly and clearly with everyone and verify that everyone knows ahead of time what's going on

Solicit feedback from residents, staff, and musicians, and listen!

Tools & Forms Charts providing detailed tasks and responsibilities
Feedback questionnaire for musicians and parents

References Zeisel, John, I'M STILL HERE, Avery, 2009. (www.ImStillHere.org)

Running the Sessions

Planning & Scheduling Performances	Complete by	Music School Director	Music Program Coordinator/Intern	Geriatric Program Director	Facility Activities Director	CNAs/Staff	Music Teacher/Group Leader	Performers
Develop initial list of teachers & performers, including contact info		X						
Select performers for first month, 3 sundowning sessions/week		X	X					
Note performers & dates for Months 2 & 3		X	X					
Place performance dates and times on monthly calendar			X		X			
Provide orientation session/training to facility staff			X	X	X	X		
Communicate performance schedule to facility staff					X			
Provide information to musicians about preparing & performing			X					
Monitor piano tuning, determine when necessary (normal, special)	Min. 3x/yr.		X					
Call piano tuner to notify & schedule		X						
Plan program, list names of pieces, composers, musicians, instruments	At least 1 week prior						X	X
Contact music teacher/leader to verify schedule & collect info	At least 1 week prior		X				X	
Confirm final details with music teacher or group leader	2 days prior		X				X	
Communicate program info to AD	At least 2-3 days prior				X			

Running the Sessions

Performance Day: Before the Session (3:30 pm Performance)

Task	Complete by	Music Program Coordinator	Music Intern	Geriatric Program Director	Facility Activities Director	CNAs/ Staff	Music Teacher/ Group Leader	Performers
Update management & staff about day's planned events	Early a.m.			X				
Notify CNAs about event & time requirements	Early a.m.			X				
Clear out performance space, rearrange furniture if necessary	2:30 p.m.		X		X			
Music program personnel arrive	2:45 p.m.		X					
Notify receptionist musicians will be arriving, page Activities Director	2:45 p.m.		X					
Remind CNAs and verify they're on schedule (shift change affects)	3:00 p.m.			X				
Residents woken, toileted, dressed	3:00 p.m.					X		
Transport residents from ward to performance space	3:15 p.m.			X	X	X		
Retrieve musical equipment from storage, set up, test	3:15 p.m.	X	X					
Prepare space for instrument cases, coats, etc.	3:15 p.m.	X	X					
Greeter out front to meet & guide performers	3:15 p.m.		X	X				
Musicians arrive & set up	3:15 p.m.						X	X

Running the Sessions

Performance Day: During the Session (3:30 pm Performance)

	Complete by	Music Program Coordinator	Music Intern	Geriatric Program Director	Facility Activities Director	CNAs/Staff	Music Teacher/Group Leader	Performers
Play introductory music as audience is brought in		▓	▓					
Give opening statement about program; Intro music leader	3:30 p.m.	▓						
Play standard opening composition	3:35 p.m.	▓	▓					
Introduce individual performers	Beginning of perf.						▓	
Introduce/describe each musical piece	Before it is performed						▓	▓
Monitor individual behaviors to head off problems & encourage	Throughout		▓	▓	▓	▓	▓	
Ensure that performers introduce themselves and compositions	Throughout	▓					▓	
Monitor audience for attention span, shorten program if needed	Throughout	▓	▓	▓				
If formal study, observe and chart individual resident responses	Throughout	▓	▓	▓				
After last piece, thank musicians, give concluding statement	No later than 4:15	▓						
Play standard closing composition	4:20	▓	▓				▓	▓

Running the Sessions

Performance Day: After the Session (3:30 pm Performance)

	Complete by	Music Program Coordinator	Music Intern	Geriatric Program Director	Facility Activities Director	CNAs/ Staff	Music Teacher/ Group Leader	Performers
If program was short, continue with additional sing-alongs, etc.	4:15 p.m.	X	X					
Distribute feedback questionnaire to music leader and parents	Immediately	X	X					
Continue playing music (live or recorded) as residents are removed	4:15 p.m.	X	X					
Return residents to rooms/ward or other designated destinations	4:30 p.m.			X	X	X		
Pack up and store all musical equipment, move piano if necessary	4:30 p.m.	X	X					
Return room furniture to required configuration	4:30 p.m.			X	X	X		
Musicians complete and return feedback questionnaires	Within 2 days						X	X
Provide informal feedback to music leader about program	Immediately	X						
Allow time for performers and audience to interact	4:30 p.m.						X	X
Conduct meetings with performers to share experience & ideas	Monthly	X					X	X

Chapter 8: Administering Your Program

Chapter Goals

Our goals in this chapter are to enable the Community Music School Executive Director to administer the Cognitive Behavior Modification through Music program in a manner that uses the school's resources most efficiently, provides the greatest educational benefits to the school's students, and builds the best possible relationships with teachers, the Alzheimer's facility, and the community.

Objectives

The information and tools provided in this chapter will help you:
- Communicate regularly about the program within the school
- Manage the Music Program Coordinator
- Build and track participation in the program by teachers, students, and other performers
- Identify trends and issues in musician participation and troubleshoot problems
- Build & monitor morale/attitude about the program
- Manage the program budget effectively

Overview   Running the sessions and running the day to day program will be the responsibility of the Music Program Coordinator. As we discussed earlier in this manual, the amount of time required on-site at the facility and the level of communications and detailed activity required will be well outside the capacity of the Executive Director.

Still, the Director is ultimately accountable for the overall administration and success of the program. If the Music School is the originator of the program and the recipient of any funding, as we have described, the Executive Director will be responsible for the program's overall management and how the program is perceived in the public eye. The program will become a highly visible extension of the school's mission and image, so making sure that it runs well and that the Music Program Coordinator is extraordinarily well-supported will be crucial.

This accountability translates to three primary areas of responsibility for the Executive Director in administering the program:
- Communication with the school community—spreading the word and listening to feedback
- Coordination and communication with the Music Program Coordinator to monitor program activities and status
- Providing and managing the resources (people and finances) the Music Program Coordinator needs in order to run a successful program

Communicating about the program   In earlier chapters (Chapter 2: Planning; Chapter 3: Facility; Chapter 5: Musicians), we discussed when and how the Executive Director should communicate about the program while initially considering the project's feasibility and while beginning implementation. To recap, some of the activities we recommended included the following:
1. Send educational materials via email to faculty and board; explain you will be beginning the process of seeking funding
2. Update everyone on progress frequently at board and faculty meetings
3. When funding is secured, call a meeting of the faculty specifically to discuss the program and what to expect; get initial sign-ups there and then
4. Send memo to all faculty describing in depth what was discussed at the meeting and urging teachers to share info with student families and to schedule a day; follow up with email
5. Send email to music school families
6. Contact music departments of local universities by phone and follow up with email; also contact local musicians with strong ties to the music school
7. After the funding has been secured and the first couple of performances have been completed, send out a press release alerting local media to the program

Communi-cating about the program, cont'd.

After the program is up and running, day to day operations and communications between the school and the facility will be handled primarily by the Music Program Coordinator. The Executive Director still needs to play a role in communicating about the program within the school at every opportunity, though, in order to make sure that the program becomes an integral part of the organization's culture. As performances continue, the Executive Director should report back frequently to the board, the faculty, and the music school community of students and parents with stories, photos, and feedback. We made a point of incorporating some discussion of the program into every board meeting and faculty meeting, and we recommend that you include at least some mention in every newsletter, catalog, and fund-raising piece that you distribute.

Displaying Program Activities

Another way of keeping the program foremost in the attention of teachers and students at your school and promoting participation would be a prominent display just inside your school's entrance. This could be a large bulletin board or very large calendar that changes monthly, showing who is scheduled to perform when. The display might also include quotes from audience members, caregivers, performers, and others that reveal the program's importance and impact. You might also include photos, or copies of publicity or articles your program has generated, and so on. The point is to have a highly visible reminder that people pass frequently. Use your imagination and invite creative input from everyone at the school!

Supervising the Music Program Coordinator

The ideal candidate for the Music Program Coordinator position will be someone who operates independently and manages time and juggles multiple tasks very well (and possesses all the other skills we described in the Position Description in Chapter 2.) The level of day-to-day oversight required from the Executive Director should be minimal; if it is not, you probably have the wrong person in the job.

The Music Program Coordinator should be encouraged to take ownership of the program. If the Coordinator is an employee of the Community Music School, as we recommended earlier, the Executive Director will naturally have the same managerial responsibilities he/she has for all other employees at the school. These will vary according to the general practices at your school. However, the Executive Director should avoid micro-managing the Coordinator. Regular meetings (twice a month) will be important to discuss challenges, successes, and improvements that can be made, and for the Director to gather the information to be reported back to the school community. The Executive Director should also attend performances as frequently as possible (at minimum once a month) to directly observe the impact on residents and to continually nourish the ties between the school and the Alzheimer's facility.

Building and tracking participation

You will need to decide at the beginning of the program who will be responsible for scheduling musicians for performances. This should be a single person who can provide a single point of contact for the musicians, and should be someone who is reachable during the school's normal hours. If the Music Program Coordinator has this role, regular reporting to the Executive Director is crucial. The Executive Director must always know when faculty and students will be representing the school in public, including who will be performing, where, and when.

In Chapter 9: Documenting Your Program, we recommend several methods for tracking program activities and results, including some suggested tools/forms for doing so. The Executive Director should read this chapter and review the tools and decide with the Music Program Coordinator which ones will be used and which ones the Executive Director wants to see regularly. The information should prove to be quite useful for the director in keeping track of who has performed, musician and audience feedback after performances, and trends in the responses of the people living with Alzheimer's.

Monitoring morale & attitudes

The Executive Director should make a point of acknowledging every teacher and student and outside musician who performs in the program. This could be done through a simple thank you when passing in the building, or through an email, phone call, or recognition at a faculty meeting. By keeping track of participation and showing constant interest and appreciation, the Executive Director helps enthusiasm remain high and can help the Music Program Coordinator succeed.

Identifying and trouble-shooting problems

Maintaining close communications with everyone from the music school who is involved in the program should enable you to spot any potential issues or problems early, before they become major issues.

Managing the program budget

Managing the budget for the Cognitive Behavior Modification through Music program shouldn't be any different from managing any other grant-funded program at the music school. The same basic, common-sense rules apply here:
- Keep on top of expenses
- Keep the responsible individual, i.e., the Music Program Coordinator, informed about the status of remaining funds
- Do not wait until funding is about to run out to find more
- Make a plan for sustaining the program between funding cycles

Cautions   Partnerships with several key players can be difficult to manage. Depending on the individuals and organizations involved, the Executive Director may also need to schedule regular meetings (every few months) that include the Music Program Coordinator and the key person from the Alzheimer's facility (probably the Geriatric Program Director, but could vary.)

Tips   Be open to new ideas about the program and give them full consideration, even after the program is up and running successfully.

                     It's important for the Executive Director to schedule ways to remain actively involved in the program so it doesn't "fall off the radar." In a busy music school environment, programs that are running smoothly, especially at a remote site, can easily slip from attention.

Tools &   See the forms provided in Chapter 9: Documenting Your Program.
Forms

References   Guttman, Jacqueline Sideman, *Partners in Excellence*, National Guild of Community Schools of the Arts, 2005.

Chapter 9: Documenting Your Program

Chapter Goals

Our goals in this chapter are to enable you to document the participation in, response to, and results of your Cognitive Behavior Modification through Music program. Good documentation will enable you to demonstrate your successes, identify any shortcomings and correct them, and contribute to the overall body of knowledge about Alzheimer's and music.

Objectives

The information and tools provided in this chapter will help the Community Music School Executive Director, Music Program Coordinator, and Geriatric Program Director

- Monitor and record participant responses and behaviors during each music session
- Identify and document longer term changes in individual mood, behavior, and cognition that may be attributable to the program
- Compile the observed results of your program
- Report on changes in residents' mood and behavior
- Identify and report on broader impacts of the program on facility staff, residents and their family members, musicians, and the Community Music School

Overview   How do you communicate your success? By documenting your results, not merely your actions. It may be of some interest to report that *x* number of musicians performed in *y* number of sessions during the first year, but these figures will mainly be of interest internally, i.e., at the community music school. What will really matter to anyone interested in supporting the program financially are the beneficial effects you can describe (and back up with specifics!) for the audience, the facility, and the musicians. At minimum this means preparing a comprehensive report annually, or at the end of each funding cycle, as mentioned in Chapter 9.

In order to prepare meaningful reports, it will be very important for you to formally document your program's participation, sessions, and results. Only by keeping regular, written records of what goes on in each performance and how the musicians, audience, and staff respond, both immediately and over time, will you know how you're doing and be able to communicate your results to others. Your documentation will help you build and maintain a strong relationship with the partnering Alzheimer's facility, identify and encourage repeat musical performers, recruit new musicians, meet the reporting requirements of your funding sources, justify new rounds of funding, and enhance the community music school's visibility and reputation in the community.

The study we conducted as part of our program in Northampton was characterized by a psychologist from Smith College as "an observational study with participation approach." In this case, the study sought to identify trends in areas such as attention, behavior, mood, and cognition of a selected group of individual residents before, during, and after performances. Although we attempted to quantify results, administrative difficulties at the facility made it very difficult to collect and record hard data consistently. Also, we did not employ control groups or attempt to isolate the effects of music from those of other potentially influencing factors. For example, the regular social interactions with more new people that were created for our audience by the program had their own impact, separate from the music itself. A more formal study might attempt to account for that and other factors such as staff turnover, type and level of cooperation from staff, changes in season, etc.

So far, there has been a real dearth of solid scientific research into the long-term effects of music on the mood, behavior, cognition, and even physical health of people living with Alzheimer's, despite increasing interest and a very real need for information. Constructing such rigorous and verifiable studies will call for the participation of professionals from the fields of psychology, medicine, and/or the social sciences, along with much greater funding than will be necessary to launch the program we describe in this manual.

Overview, cont'd.

While we are certainly interested in pursuing this more formal type of study, that kind of research is beyond the scope of this manual. However, you may be able to identify interested researchers in your area who will work with you and use this manual as a foundation for developing a more sophisticated research project that will engender a substantive contribution to knowledge in the field of Alzheimer's research. If you do, we would be very interested in hearing from you.

The remainder of this chapter describes how we recommend documenting and reporting your program's activities and results in order to meet the information needs of the various stakeholders and assure the program's ongoing success. We include some sample forms for charting individual responses, for collecting feedback from performers, for identifying monthly trends in participants, and for capturing other useful information.

How and when should you keep records?

At minimum, we recommend that you keep these written records:
- During each performance:
  - Chart responses of selected individuals to each composition
  - Summarize the response of the overall audience of residents and staff to the performance (attention, mood, behaviors, cognition)
  - After close, solicit reactions and feedback from performers using a questionnaire
- Monthly:
  - Summarize program activities (Number of performances, performers, types of music, general responses of audience to each performance, etc.)
  - Summarize responses of each selected individual to the previous month's performances
  - For the same selected individuals, assess longer-term trends in mood, behavior, cognition & medication, sleeping and eating, and other factors the facility may be interested in tracking. This information can be gained through consultation with medical staff, CNAs, activities staff, and others as needed.

Who should document your program?

Primary responsibility for assuring that your program is adequately documented rests with the Music Program Coordinator. The Coordinator won't be able to complete all of the necessary observation and record-keeping alone, however; others will need to assist in observing residents during and after performances and charting their responses. (This is one of many areas where an intern will be very helpful.) You may also ask other facility staff to help out with tracking behaviors and responses during performances. Try to maintain consistency in who helps with this responsibility so that your data remains as reliable as possible.

Who should document your program?, cont'd.

Assessing longer term trends for each of the individual participants will require some significant cooperation and participation from facility staff, especially the Geriatric Program Director and the Director of Nursing. Privacy concerns and confidentiality issues will probably prevent the Music Program Coordinator from directly reviewing any person's records without special authorization from the facility's administration and permission from a family member or other individual empowered to allow the review. Even if the Music Program Coordinator is able to directly view medical records, identities will need to be shielded when reporting results.

Because of these obstacles, you will be best served by establishing with the Geriatric Program Director and the Director of Nursing at the beginning of the program the kinds of observations and information you need in order to identify longer term effects. Review the sample forms provided in this chapter, then agree on your specific approach, responsibilities, and schedule. Tracking this information should also be to the benefit of these administrators, as they will have the best interests of the residents in mind and will want to be assured that the program is beneficial. They will probably also want to use the same information in their own reporting to the facility's senior management.

When and what should you report?

Your reporting needs will be driven by your own particular situation. Depending on who funds your program, the information needs of your Community Music School's Board and the Alzheimer's facility's management, bookkeeping schedules, and so on, you may need to provide different levels of information to different groups at different times.

At the most general level, we recommend that you compile and report your results at all significant milestones, such as the end of a funding cycle, or the end of the school year, etc. We suggest that you include the following information:

- Roll up an aggregate summary of program sessions (Number of sessions, number of performers, etc.)
- Update program budget figures
- Summarize feedback you have collected from musicians, teachers, and parents after each performance during the period
- Summarize longer-term trends in areas such as mood, behavior, cognition, eating and sleep patterns, and medication for the selected participants, based on monthly assessments while protecting confidentiality
- Feedback from facility staff, including medical, CNAs, activities, and others illustrating their attitudes toward the program and identifying any general changes they have observed in residents or the facility that they attribute to the music program. (Questionnaires were not useful with this audience, because all members are quite busy, have higher priorities, or may have language issues that prevent them from completing written answers. We had more success asking questions and writing down the answers.)

Key People & Required Support

- Geriatric Program Director—assists with charting responses of selected individuals during performances; assures completion of monthly assessments of individuals

- Activities Director—assists with charting responses of selected individuals during performances; assures completion of monthly assessments of individuals

- Director of Nursing—collects comments and impressions from CNAs; assures completion of monthly assessments of individuals

Cautions

- When documenting and reporting, always be respectful of individual privacy and be aware of medical confidentiality issues.

- Remember, once you put something in writing, It assumes a life of its own and you may not be able to control who sees it later.

- Keep everything as simple as possible; don't try to put any additional paperwork on facility staff, especially CNAs!

Tips

- Determine at the beginning of your program the reporting that you will need to do, so you can make sure that collect the information you need while the sessions are running. Trying to prepare reports by remembering or recreating information from events that occurred months ago never works, and will likely cost you more time and frustration than simply keeping the records in the first place.

- Don't overburden the facility staff with new forms and additional paperwork. The caregivers who work directly with your audience members are already required to complete many forms and fill in records daily. Instead, the Music Program Coordinator must assume responsibility for all program-related records and reports. Try to get permission to review notes the CNAs or others are already making about trends in individual status, or work with the Geriatric Program Director or someone in a similar role to have the highlights summarized for you without identifying information.

**Tools &
Forms**

- Session observation chart for individuals (2 samples of different approaches we tried)
- Session reaction form for group
- Performer questionnaire
- Monthly assessment of participant trends for selected individuals
- Monthly summary of program activities

References   See sample reports on the Northampton Community Music Center's website (www.ncmc.net) under Alzheimer's Project.

Cognitive Behavior Modification through Music Program
Session Observation Chart for Individuals (Sample 1)

Name of song	Mood-E/L	Language S/T/M	Eyes O/C	Fingers L/R	Hand O/C-T/CI	Arm-L/R	Head movement	Leg L/R	Getting up	Interaction
STAR SPANGLED (A)										
(B)										
(C)										
(D)										
(E)										
(F)										
(G)										
(H)										
TIL WE AGAIN										
COMMENTS										

Entertainer _____

DATE _____

KEY: LT-LEFT R-RIGHT O-OPEN C-CLOSED CL-CLAPPING TP-TAPPING S-SINGING T-TALKING M-MOUTH MOVEMENT E-ENTER L-LEAVING.

Cognitive Behavior Modification through Music Program
Session Observation Chart for Individuals (Sample 2)

Date:

Performer:

Patient	Language		Mouthing words	Finger movements (tapping, snapping)	Hand movements (tapping, clapping)	Arm movements (conducting)	Foot movements (tapping)	Leg movements	Getting up	Participation (if applicable)
	Singing	Talking								
A										
B										
C										
D										
E										
F										
G										

Cognitive Behavior Modification through Music Program
Session Reaction Form for Group

<u>Music Coordinator</u>: Use this form to summarize the response of the <u>overall</u> audience of residents and staff to each performance after the performance has ended and musicians and audience have left. Attach this form, the completed musician questionnaire (next page), and a copy of the program to create a record of each performance.

Date of performance<u>:</u>_____ Leader's name:_____

Age range of performers (circle):   10 or younger   Teens   Adults

Type of music (e.g., classical, jazz, Broadway, 50s popular, etc.):_____

Rate each of the following (1 is lowest, 5 is highest)

	Low		Med		High
	1	**2**	**3**	**4**	**5**
1. Level of audience attention to the performance					
2. Mood of audience before performance					
3. Mood of audience after performance					
4. Level of musician interaction with audience (How much did the musicians engage?)					
5. Level of audience engagement with performers (How much did audience talk to musicians?)					

What were the notable successes of this performance?

What were the challenges of this performance?

Other comments?

Cognitive Behavior Modification through Music Program
Performer Questionnaire

<u>Music Coordinator</u>: Distribute to music teacher/group leader after performance

<u>Performer</u>: Your feedback is very important for helping us make sure the program works as well as possible. Please complete this feedback form and return it to the Music Coordinator before leaving, if possible.

<u>Performer's name</u>:

<u>Date of performance</u>:

1. How did you hear about this project?

2. What did you take away from being part of this project?

3. Please comment on your performance experience today, including any responses from residents

4. How did the actual performance experience differ from what you expected it to be?

5. What suggestions do you have?

6. Based on your experience today, would you volunteer to perform in this program again?

7. What other performers would you recommend for participation in this program? (Please provide name and any contact information you can.)

Cognitive Behavior Modification through Music Program
Monthly Assessment of Participant Trends

<u>Music Coordinator</u>: Use this form to summarize the monthly changes in each of the selected people you are monitoring in your program. Complete a separate form for each resident each month. Work with the Geriatric Program Director and Director of Nursing to assess each individual.

Patient ID:_____   Date (MM/YY):_____

Rate each of the following (1 is worse, 5 is better)

The individual's general level over the previous month:	Worse 1	2	Same 3	4	Better 5
1. Agitation					
2. Anxiety					
3. Aggression					
4. Apathy					
5. Clarity					

Have the individual's eating habits changed over the past month, especially on the evenings after musical performances? If so, how?

Has the individual's need for PRNs for agitation during sundowning changed over the past month? If so, how?

Have the individual's sleep patterns changed over the past month, especially on the evenings after musical performances? If so, how?

What other changes have been observed in this individual?

Who attended this assessment session?

Cognitive Behavior Modification through Music Program
Monthly Summary of Program Sessions

Music Coordinator: Use this form to keep track of basic details about the music sessions every month. Keeping regular summaries will make your reporting much easier.

Date (MM/YY): _____   Total Number of performances this month: _____

Date	Performer	# in Audience	High Points	Challenges

Chapter 10: Sustaining Your Program

Chapter Goals

Our goals in this chapter are to enable you to sustain your Cognitive Behavior Modification through Music program and expand on its success over time.

Objectives

The information and tools provided in this chapter will help the Community Music School Executive Director:
- identify potential funding sources to cover ongoing program expenses
- assure participation by many musicians over time
- maintain a strong, positive long-term relationship with the Alzheimer's facility
- publicize the program locally to foster local participation and funding for the program and enhanced visibility for the Community Music School and all of its programs
- evaluate the pros and cons of expanding the program to more than one facility

Overview

The Cognitive Behavior Modification through Music program can be very effective during its first year, but needs more time to flourish. The more successful your program is during its first year, the better your chances of sustaining the effort across multiple years. And you must be able to communicate your accomplishments! In Chapter 9: Documenting Your Program, we discussed the importance of keeping regular records and of reporting **results** rather than simply summarizing actions. Effectively communicating your program's successes to potential supporters will depend on providing readily available proof of its beneficial impacts on all concerned.

The keys to sustaining your program over time will include:
- securing ongoing funding through sustaining contributors and/or new sponsors
- keeping a strong core of musicians involved, and continually bringing in new performers
- fostering the best possible long-term relationship with the facility staff and administration through active communication
- publicizing the program locally as often as possible
- considering very carefully whether or not it makes sense to expand the program once your success becomes more widely known

We'll discuss each of these concepts in the remainder of this chapter.

Identifying Ongoing Funding

As any Executive Director knows, obtaining the initial funding to implement a program such as this one can be very difficult, especially during tight economic times. But it is easier to secure funding for a new and innovative program (particularly a partnership) than it is to secure funding for an existing program. So how can you secure ongoing funding?

First, you should always think about how you can keep the program exciting and fresh for potential new grantors. Part of doing so will depend on being able to communicate your results clearly and powerfully (yes, we're being repetitive, but this is important.) Local publicity will also help.

Foundations rarely fund the same program twice. If you have the opportunity at the outset to apply for a multi-year grant, that should obviously be your priority.

Budget generously in pilot years and figure out where costs can be cut in later years so the program could be sustainable with less if necessary.

Keep an eye out for private donors who take a particular interest in the program—invite them to see the sessions in progress, and then later, maybe you can ask them to help subsidize the program.

Partnering with a Facility for Funding

Healthcare facilities in the U.S. are either for-profit or not-for-profit. Many middle to late-stage Alzheimer's Dementia residents live in for-profit Medicaid/Medicare facilities that are struggling financially; many of these residents receive a minimum of care and attention. In your area you may find that the population most in need of this program lives in such a facility. Opportunities to apply for joint funding with for-profit facilities may be difficult or impossible, however, because few funding sources are available that will support it.

Consider investigating not-for-profit facilities; although non-profit facilities have found grants more difficult to obtain over the past several years, opportunities do exist. By partnering with a non-profit facility, you may improve your overall chances of securing funding for the program. If you do take this approach, as always, it will be very important to clearly define roles and responsibilities at the proposal stage.

Keeping Musicians Involved

We have invested a substantial number of words earlier in this manual regarding how you can recruit performers for your program, both within the school and from the larger community. One of the most critical points to reiterate here is that the sessions will take place during prime lesson hours for your music teachers, and that participating in the sessions could result in a loss of income for them. The two main strategies we've discussed for addressing this issue were to provide a stipend through grant funding and to help the teachers make the performances a part of their regular teaching schedule, such as making the sessions practice recitals for groups of their students.

Recognition and appreciation will also play a major role in keeping musicians involved. Whenever a musician participates, even if it's for the fifth or tenth time, she or he should hear a word of thanks or receive a public pat on the back from the music school's leadership and the Music Program Coordinator. Remember, the musicians are the people who will ultimately make your program succeed or fail. Without their enthusiastic cooperation, you've got nothing to offer!

Maintaining Good Ties With the Facility

Your partnering Alzheimer's facility will not remain static while you get your program up and running, and the longer you run, the more changes you will see. Personnel will change at all levels. Ownership of the facility may change. The population of residents and their concerned family members will certainly change. In every case, it will be very important for the Music Program Coordinator and Executive Director to be able to communicate clearly and effectively what the program is, how it works, and how it has been effective for everyone involved. Over time you will certainly build up a core of supporters within the facility who can help you communicate with new personnel. But your responsibility for presenting, even "selling" the program within the facility will always be necessary at some level.

Again, this is an area where keeping consistent records and preparing regular, timely reports on results will make the job easiest and serve the participants and the music school best. The Music Program Coordinator needs to remain aware of changes in personnel at the facility and to be active and positive in educating new people about the program.

For example, if you hear that a new administrator has joined the facility, or a new Director of Nursing or Medical Director, try to schedule an appointment as soon as possible to introduce yourself and the program, rather than waiting for this new person to hear about the sessions from someone without your depth of understanding and experience. That way you can make sure the message is delivered correctly: this program is not entertainment, it's not an activity, like Bingo or regular karaoke hour—it's a part of the regime for the residents living with Alzheimer's and should be viewed as an important part of their regular non-pharmacological treatment for alleviation of symptoms.

Active communication is the key, as always in this program. If you leave the description up to others, you have no way of ensuring that the information delivered will be accurate or supportive.

Publicizing the Program

Securing local publicity for your program should be an ongoing effort from the time you first establish a partnership and secure funding. Many people are very interested in Alzheimer's dementia now because of the growth of the number of people diagnosed and the related publicity. Any local program that promises some alleviation of symptoms, especially through the arts, will be a natural interest for local newspapers, television, and radio. Your community music school may already have contacts at local media outlets and standard ways of generating coverage.

This program should be an integral, even leading, part of your overall local publicity campaign through a regular schedule of press releases for significant events and milestones and through efforts to generate more detailed and prominent feature coverage. Many Alzheimer's facility will be happy to partner with you in these efforts, especially through their marketing staff.

Involving Local Researchers

The Cognitive Behavior Modification Through Music program is a music and medical partnership that incorporates recent scientific discoveries about music, brain function, and Alzheimer's Dementia. Because of its musical and medical nature and the very broad interest in these topics, the program could offer fertile territory for additional research. Additional research into the results of the program could be suitable for:

- Senior thesis
- Research projects
- Master's Thesis
- Doctoral Dissertation

For example, a research might compare results of doing this program at sun-downing time with other times of day.

In the areas of cognition and behavior, we have observed that music sessions have transformed resident behaviors—and at the same time ignited areas of thought, memory, and communication assumed gone forever. These observations prompt a call for aligning research in specific areas affecting resident sleep, eating, and medication.

Music sessions have also increased knowledge, learning, understanding, attitude, interest, for participants, families, staff, and possibly the community as a whole, and additional research could substantiate the broader educational and societal impacts of similar programs.

This type of research partnership may provide additional ways of connecting your program and your school with your larger community through more formal relationships with local higher education institutions. All partners would benefit, as would the residents.

Pros and Cons of Expanding the Program

Once information about your program and its success begin to circulate locally, you may begin to hear from other local facilities. Not only is the need great for this type of program, but in some areas the market for nursing homes and similar facilities may be quite competitive. Your program may be perceived as an offering that provides not only a real benefit to residents, but also a marketing advantage to facilities that are eager to keep their occupancy up.

As tempting as it may be to expand your program into multiple facilities, we recommend extreme caution here. You have seen by now that this program requires a great deal of intense and coordinated work. Stretching resources such as the Music Program Coordinator and the pool of performers across multiple sites could be detrimental to your original program and will make the success of additional programs much more difficult to achieve.

Simply consider the logistics of scheduling and conducting two or three live performances per week at two locations! Because the Music Program Coordinator must facilitate every session, this would mean sessions six days a week—or you'd need to hire an additional Music Program Coordinator for the second program. While your organization may have the resources to do so, then consider whether you would have enough musicians available to fill both schedules. You might even find your two Music Program Coordinators competing with each other to book musicians.

But as we said, the need is great. If your school has the resources and funding to support more than one program, AFTER YOU HAVE SUCCESSFULLY IMPLEMENTED ONE PROGRAM, you should by all means do so.

Conclusion   Our aim in this manual has been to provide you with as much practical, hands-on advice as we can, along with many opinions based on our own experience. The Cognitive Behavior Modification through Music program has been an outstanding experience for us, one that has reinforced our deep beliefs in the powers of music to connect people of all ages and backgrounds, able to bring even the most isolated among us into community. We hope the background and tools that we offer in this book can help community music schools everywhere build similar programs.

In some cases, we've described how we should have done things based on our trial and error experience, or we offer an approach we arrived at by the conclusion of two funding cycles rather than where we began. So take the advice and tools we've presented as your starting point for your own program. Your school's staffing, financial resources, teachers and students and your area's Alzheimer's facilities will be different from ours, so you'll need to modify our approach to make it our own.

As you launch your own program, we would very much like to hear about what works for you and what doesn't. We'd like to hear your new ideas and new approaches so that we can continue to nourish our own efforts and share the information with a wider audience.

We intend to provide regular updates and new information as it becomes available, so please be sure to check back often at the website for the Northampton Community Music Center (www.ncmc.net) where the Alzheimer's project has its own page. You will also find this manual downloadable there as a PDF and a link where you can send us any feedback you have about this manual.

Bibliography

Books

Boyer, Johann Misey. *Creativity Matters: The Arts and Aging Toolkit*. New York: National Guild of Community Schools of the Arts, 2007. www.nationalguild.org

Cohen, Gene D. *The Mature Mind: The Positive Power of the Aging Brain*. New York: Basic Books, 2005. www.creativeaging.org

Cohen, Gene D. *The Creative Age: Awakening Human Potential in the Second Half of Life*. New York: Harper Collins Publishers, 2000. www.creativeaging.org

Doidge, Norman. *The Brain That Changes Itself*. New York: Penguin Books, 2007.

Guttman, Jacqueline Sideman. *Partners in Excellence.* New York: National Guild of Community Schools of the Arts, 2005. www.nationalguild.org

Halpern, Sue. *Can't Remember What I Forgot: Your Memory, Your Mind, Your Future.* New York: Harmony Books, 2008.

Levitin, Daniel J. *The World In Six Songs: How The Musical Brain Created Human Nature.* New York: Plume Books, 2008.

Levitin, Daniel J. *This Is Your Brain On Music: The Science of a Human Obsession.* New York: Plume Books, 2007. www.yourbrainonmusic.com

Mace, Nancy L. & Rabins, Peter V. *The 36-Hour Day, 4th Edition*. Baltimore: The Johns Hopkins University Press, 2006.

Sacks, Oliver. *Musicophilia: Tales of Music and the Brain.* New York: Vintage Books, 2008. http://musicophilia.com

Shenk, David, *The Forgetting: Alzheimer's: Portrait Of An Epidemic*. New York: Anchor Books, 2003. davidshenk.com

Zeisel, John. *I'm Still Here*. New York: Avery, 2009. www.ImStillHere.org

Websites

The Alzheimer's Association, www.alz.org

McGovern Institute for Brain Research at MIT, web.mit.edu/mcgovern

Society for the Arts in Health Care, www.thesah.org

Society for Neuroscience, www.sfn.org (*Brain Plasticity and Alzheimer's Disease*)

Acknowledgements

First and foremost, we extend our utmost gratitude to the F.A.O. Schwarz Family Foundation, which funded the two-year Cognitive Behavior Modification Through Music program and the development, printing, and distribution of this manual. Without their very generous support, the project would not have been possible.

Beverly Pickering wishes to acknowledge the following colleagues with outstanding vision who contributed their expertise in the fields of music and health over a span of years in the Boston area. Our work together on innovative projects provided the foundation for this successful partnership in Northampton, Massachusetts.

- Paul Broadnax, Anna Taylor Caleb, Richard G. Conti, Peter Kontrimas, Martha Ann Robert, Lucien G. Robert, P. Jacquelyn Schmidt, Caroline Schwarz-Schastny, Madeline Sifantus, Visiting Nurse Association Care Network of Boston & Hospice, Margaret Wailes.

Beverly also wishes to acknowledge Dr. Gene Cohen and Ruth McCaffrey, the very special people whose insight, advice, and encouragement bolstered her determination to initiate the partnership project, and Jillian Anderson, Alicia DePaolo, and Esther Park, Smith College interns who helped so very much with running the program. Michele Wick also provided very helpful advice on structuring the observational methods and tools we used.

Jason Trotta wishes to acknowledge the many people at the Northampton Community Music Center and elsewhere who played a role in supporting the project and helping it run smoothly, including:

- Bill Wallace, who kept the piano tuned
- Meg Kelsey Wright and the Board of Directors of Northampton Community Music Center
- Administrative Staff of the Northampton Community Music Center: Katherine Davis, Lindsay Hobbs, Lita Robinson, and Daniel Schwartz
- Hampshire College & Smith College Interns: Jordan Crouser, Jessica DeBruin, Mike Doyle, Sora Harris-Vincent
- Jonathan Herman, Kenneth Cole, and everyone at the National Guild for Community Arts Education

We all extend our thanks to the many staff members at the Northampton Rehabilitation & Nursing Center: Josie Zawada for outstanding teamwork. Timothy Barnes, Janice Batura, Steve Burnham, Deborah Clark, Brenda Colon, Julia Blakeney Hayward, James Lomastro, Gretchen Milks, Rich Perry, Meghan Reusch, Rockwell CNA staff, Jennifer Wade, Ed Walsh and facility receptionists.

Thanks also to Reverend Madeleine Sifantus, who provided a beautiful new Schimmel upright piano that had belonged to Eleanor Burgess, a devoted Golden Tones member who died suddenly just after purchasing the instrument.

Thanks to the people who reviewed the final draft of this manual to help us make sure it would help others build from our experience: Marigene Kettler, Ian Blake Newhem, Catherine Barufaldi, and Sarah Winawer-Wetzel.

And very special thanks to the many musicians who made the program a success:

Music Teachers & Students
- Bruce Diehl & Amherst College Jazz Ensemble
- Donna Gouger & brass ensemble
- Emily Greene & Suzuki violin students
- Jane Hanson & vocal students
- Holly Havis & piano students
- Kitty Hay & flute students
- Lynn Lovell & bass students
- Kate O'Connor & piano students
- Christine Olson & piano students
- Monica Robelotto & piano students
- Tom Slowick, Gary Smulyen & Berkshire Hills Music Academy students
- Anne Werry & Suzuki cello students
- Meg Kelsey Wright & Piano Connection
- Daniel Kim-Amherst College a cappella

A capella & accompanied vocal groups
- Impeachments (a cappella)
- Paradise City Singers
- Donald Kim and Route 9 (Amherst College a cappella)
- Sabrinas (Amherst College a cappella)
- Smiffenpoofs (Smith College a cappella)
- Terra Irradient (Amherst College a cappella)
- Vibes (Smith College a cappella)

Individual performers & instrumental groups
- Kismet Al-Hussaini
- Julia Bady
- Richard Bauer
- Carolyn Bell
- Lauren Bell
- Paul Broadnax
- Winnie Brown
- Joseph Blumenthal

- Ellen Clegg
- Richard Conti
- Sam Coates-Finke
- Duo Fusion: Sarah Swersey and Joe Belmont
- Claudia Eitner
- Deborah Gilwood
- Evelyn Harris
- Carol Hutter
- Colleen Jennings
- John Mason
- Louis Matias
- Mary Ellen Miller
- Yaeko Miranda
- Richard Moulding
- Northampton Flute Trio: Sue Kurian, George Owens, Jim Weber
- Stephen Page
- Matthew Quayle
- The Ramsey Family
- Rev. Madeleine Sifantus
- Richard Unsworth

Additional thanks to the University of Massachusetts Amherst Neuroscience Club, who joined the effort after the grants had ended. They engaged the residents with music and other activities and created sessions that helped everyone in the room feel better.

About the Authors

Pam Hamberg has been working with elders professionally since 1995 in various settings. She began at an adult day health center working with participants ranging from 18-80 years old in a social setting, providing stimulation through activity involvement. She then moved on to managing a milieu therapy program at a facility housing dually diagnosed residents with mental and physical limitations. Most recently she has worked as an Alzheimer's program director running the day to day operations of a forty-one bed unit.

George Owens is a writer and trainer who has designed and developed communications and training for many corporate and non-profit clients since 1981. He completed his M.F.A. at the University of Massachusetts, Amherst, and has been a working musician for four decades, playing saxophones in jazz groups and flutes from concert to contrabass with the Northampton Flutes for the past eight years. His novel, *The Judas Pool*, was published by Putnam. You can find more information about this project and his ongoing research and writing about music and Alzheimer's at www.musicandalzheimers.org.

Beverly Pickering is an R.N. and pianist with degrees from St. Olaf College and Yale. She is a member of the team of three who initiated and developed the Cognitive Behavior Modification Through Music program described in this guide. In addition, she has devoted her skills as a concert chamber artist and Registered Nurse to developing a successful music/medical program for children 5-16 years of age who had been hospitalized due to severely disturbed emotional states and violent behavior. She also performed and recorded a two-disc CD of piano compositions and donated all proceeds as a fund raiser for Visiting Nurse Care Network of Boston. Beverly was also the accompanist for the Wayland Golden Tones, whose mission of bringing music into poorly served facilities brought a special commendation from the National Council for the Arts.

Jason Trotta attended New York University, where he studied Screenwriting and Music Business & Technology, and received his Bachelor of Fine Arts degree in Music, Studio Composition from the State University of New York, Purchase College. Early in his career, Jason worked in Promotions & Marketing at A&M Records and was the Assistant Manager of a record store in Greenwich, CT. Jason joined the faculty of the Rockland Conservatory of Music in 1993, where he taught music theory and composition and was eventually hired as its Registrar. Jason was later promoted to Assistant Director at Rockland Conservatory, where he was instrumental in helping the organization secure a new home after an abrupt eviction and triple its student enrollment in just three years. Since 2003, Jason has served as the Executive Director of the Northampton Community Music Center in Northampton, MA. He continues to compose, arrange, and produce music on a freelance basis, and has had his music featured in television shows, commercials, and films around the world.